THE JEWISH QUARTERLY

The Jewish Quarterly is published four times a year
by The Jewish Quarterly Pty Ltd

Publisher: Morry Schwartz

ISBN 9781760645403 E-ISBN 9781743823910
ISSN 0449010X E-ISSN 23262516

With courtesy of the YIVO Institute for Jewish Research
www.yivo.org

Introduction © Samuel D. Kassow 2024
Translation © Solon Beinfeld 2024

Subscriptions 1 year print & digital (4 issues): £55 GBP | $75 USD.
1 year digital only: £35 GBP | $45 USD. Payment may be made
by Mastercard or Visa. Payment includes postage and handling.

Subscribe online at jewishquarterly.com or email subscribe@jewishquarterly.com
Correspondence should be addressed to: The Editor, The Jewish Quarterly,
22–24 Northumberland Street, Collingwood VIC 3066 Australia
Phone +61 3 9486 0288 Email enquiries@jewishquarterly.com

The Jewish Quarterly is published under licence from the
Jewish Literary Trust Limited, which exercises a governance function.

UK Company Number: 01189861. UK Charity Commission Number: 268589.

Printed and bound in the UK by Bell & Bain Ltd, Glasgow. The paper used
to produce this book comes from wood grown in sustainable forests.

Issue 258, November 2024

THE JEWISH QUARTERLY

The Rudashevski diary

Solon Beinfeld is Professor Emeritus of History at Washington University in St Louis. He is an active Yiddish translator and co-editor-in-chief of the *Comprehensive Yiddish–English Dictionary*.

Samuel D. Kassow is the Charles H. Northam Professor of History at Trinity College. His books include *Who Will Write Our History?*, which received the Orbis Prize of the AAASS and was a finalist for a National Jewish Book Award.

Yitskhok Rudashevski was born in Vilna on 10 December 1927 and died in October 1943.

Introduction

Samuel D. Kassow

Yitskhok Rudashevski was one of the more than one million Jewish children and young people murdered in the Holocaust. He started to write his Vilna Ghetto diary when he was fourteen. The Germans killed him in October 1943. He had not reached his sixteenth birthday.

Yitskhok did not live long enough to marry, start a family or choose a profession. What we know of him is what we read in the diary. Faced with the helplessness and humiliation of ghetto life, he fought hard to stave off depression and despair. On his fifteenth birthday he wrote: "Today I turned fifteen and live very much for tomorrow. I do not feel two ways about it. I see before me sun and sun and sun …" (10 December 1942)

But, inevitably, there were darker moods as well. In the ghetto he fell back on the inner resources he had absorbed from his family, from his teachers in the Yiddish secular schools he had attended, and from what Jews called "*nusakh Vilne*" – the values and the traditions of his native city, Vilna. Yitskhok's Jewishness had little to do with traditional religion or Zionism. In the circles that nurtured him, home was Eastern Europe, not Zion. The Jewish language was Yiddish, not Hebrew, and the Jewish future depended on a new era based on socialism and universal brotherhood. Or so he hoped.

This faith in the ultimate triumph of justice was both praiseworthy and flawed. In the face of poverty and antisemitism, Vilna's Jews created a vibrant community. They nurtured and educated dedicated and remarkable youngsters like Yitskhok Rudashevski. But they were always at the mercy of others, be they Poles, Lithuanians, Germans or Russians. What they lacked was control over their own fate.

Yitskhok tried to make the best of his life in the ghetto. As long as he could, he worked hard, studied and read. And because he wrote so well his diary is not just a valuable historical document but also a literary work in its own right. We will never know who he might have become. The many young lives cut short serve as a constant reminder of the enormity of the crime.

i

Yitskhok's diary survived thanks to his first cousin Sarah Voloshin. Yitskhok's mother and Sarah's father were brother and sister. Sarah and Yitskhok went to the same school, and their fathers both worked at Vilna's premier Yiddish daily, the *Vilner Tog*. The families were part of Vilna's secular Yiddish intelligentsia.

The collapse of Poland in 1939, the Soviet occupation of Lithuania in 1940 and the German attack on the USSR in June 1941 totally upended their lives. Forced into the tiny Vilna Ghetto in September 1941, they somehow held on for two years. When the Germans finally liquidated what was left of the Vilna Ghetto on 23 September 1943, Yitskhok's family, along with Sarah's mother and sister and four other Jews, went to ground in a "*maline*", ghetto slang for a hiding place. Sarah's father had been deported to a Nazi camp in Estonia a month before. These ten Jews held out in the *maline* for eleven days. But once their food and water gave out, they didn't stand a chance. When someone left to fetch water, Lithuanians discovered the hideout. Their fate was sealed: a stop-over at the Lukishki Prison and then a one-way trip to the shooting pits of the nearby Ponary forest.

As the truck approached Lukishki, Sarah's mother begged her to escape. She refused, but her mother insisted. Just as the truck reached the prison, Sarah jumped off and ran into a nearby passageway. The others, including Yitskhok, perished in Ponary. Sarah remembered that those final days had left Yitskhok depressed and resigned. He told her that he was ready to join his grandmother, whom the Germans had murdered in 1941. He missed her greatly, and made no effort to flee.

Sarah slipped into a nearby Jewish labour camp and then reached a Jewish partisan unit in the Rudniki Forest. When the Red Army captured Vilna in July 1944, Sarah, the only survivor of her family, returned to the hiding place to look for a family photo album that she had left there. As a friend held a ladder, she climbed up to the *maline* and rummaged underneath the dirt floor. She found the album and then her fingers touched a small notebook, which she immediately recognised as her cousin's diary.

After the war, Sarah gave the diary to the Yiddish poets and former partisans Avrom Sutzkever and Shmerke Kaczerginski, who were trying to restart some semblance of Jewish life in Vilna: a Jewish museum, a library, a school, an orphanage. But they soon saw that the Soviets were determined to destroy any vestiges of Jewish culture that had survived the war. As David Fishman shows in his important book *The Book Smugglers*, once Sutzkever and Kaczerginski understood that they had no future in Vilna, they began to smuggle precious documents and artefacts out of Soviet Lithuania, and themselves left the USSR in 1946. Most of the documents they spirited out, including Yitskhok's diary, reached the YIVO (the Yiddish Scientific Institute) in its new home in New York and are now housed in its Sutzkever–Kaczerginski Collection.

After the war Sarah stayed in Soviet Vilna, studied law and married Mordecai Klibatz. Thanks to their pre-war Polish citizenship, the couple were able to leave the USSR for Poland in 1957 and arrived in Israel in 1959. They settled in Jerusalem and had two children. Sarah worked at Yad Vashem for over fifty years, using her command of many languages to translate and prepare documents for trials of Nazi criminals. For years she tried, unsuccessfully, to persuade YIVO to return the diary to her so she could donate it to Yad Vashem. Sarah Voloshin Klibatz died in Israel in 2020.

ii

Before the war, 60,000 Jews lived in Vilna, known throughout the Jewish world as the "Jerusalem of Lithuania". The city made an outsized contribution to Jewish culture and political life. *Nusakh Vilne*, the "Vilna way", combined respect for Jewish tradition with an embrace of modernity. Vilna was the birthplace of the great eighteenth-century sage Reb Eliyahu, the "Vilna Gaon" (1720–1797), but also of the Jewish Labour Bund. Between the wars, Jewish Vilna was a world unto itself, with youth movements, four daily Yiddish newspapers and a far-flung network of clubs and voluntary associations.

In 1937 Zalmen Reyzen, the editor of the *Vilner Tog*, wrote that Vilna was "the mother city of Jewish civic life (*gezelshaft-lekhkayt*)". What he meant was that Vilna was a model for Jews everywhere. It embodied the possibility of a creative national existence in the Diaspora: a community that could counterbalance political conflict with civic responsibility, neutralise the threat of assimilation with a commitment to a Jewish language, and fund and support social institutions that embodied a deep-rooted sense of national responsibility. One might also say that Vilna was the right size: a city, not a shtetl, but much smaller than metropolises like Warsaw or Lódź. There were enough Jews to build a civic culture, but not so many that they were strangers to each other. And, crucially, there was much less social distance between various sectors of the community in Vilna than in Warsaw or Kraków.

In 1925 a new centre of Yiddish scholarship, the Yiddish Scientific Institute, was established in Vilna, which many Jews regarded as the virtual capital of an imaginary country that spanned the globe: Yiddishland. In Galicia and central Poland, Yiddish was rapidly losing ground to Polish. But in Vilna it still reigned supreme. Six times more Jews lived in Warsaw but it was Vilna that supported Poland's only Yiddish-language secondary school, the famed Realgymnasium, where Yitskhok and Sarah both studied. The Yiddish literary critic Nahum Shtif remarked that "Peretz wrote in Warsaw. But he was read in Vilna."

In the YIVO, Jewish scholarship no longer focused on the rabbis and the intellectual elites but also studied the lives of ordinary Jews: women, workers, children. In his well-known poem "Vilna", written in 1926, the poet Moyshe Kulbak wrote that *Yidish iz der proster krantz fun demben bleter oyf di arayngangen di heylik vokhige fun shtot*" (Yiddish is the homely crown of oak leaves, over the gates, sacred and profane into the city). To be sure, not all Jews in Vilna were secular Yiddishists. Religious Jews, traditional Jews and Zionists were probably in the majority. But Yiddish was the common language of the community and it was as a centre of secular Yiddishism that interwar Vilna was truly unique.

Secular Yiddish Vilna had many pillars: the YIVO; Reyzen's newspaper; the Yung Vilne literary group, which included Shmerke Kaczerginski, Avrom Sutzkever, Chaim Grade and other writers and poets; a rich musical and theatrical life. But the pride and joy of Yiddish Vilna were the secular schools.

Before the war, the schools were like a second home and its teachers were like surrogate parents. In the ghetto, as Yitskhok's diary shows, they became more important than ever. Yitskhok attended the elementary school of the Realgymnasium and studied one year in the high school before the war began. The teachers not only inculcated a deep love of Yiddish literature but also encouraged the students to reach out to Yiddish writers and to see them as friends and mentors, not remote celebrities. In 1938 Yitskhok, Sarah and other students, at the urging of their teacher Mire Bershteyn, began a correspondence with the great Yiddish poet Mani Leyb, who had been born in Ukraine and lived in New York. Their letters are now in the YIVO archives.

Since the Polish state did not recognise the Realgymnasium's diplomas until the late 1930s, students had to be especially motivated to choose it. It was considered to be close to the Bund, although several of the teachers had communist leanings. The Realgymnasium had high standards, especially in the natural sciences and mathematics. Its students were accepted to universities all over Europe. Each afternoon after classes there were clubs where students rehearsed plays, discussed books, did science experiments or planned weekend hikes. History students prepared "trials" which argued the pros and cons of major historical events. As we see in Yitskhok's diary, these trials became important in the ghetto. Were figures such as Herod and Josephus, who had collaborated with the Romans, guilty or not guilty? Did they collaborate to help their people or did they betray the Jews? Everybody understood that they were really judging the conduct of the Jewish commandant of the ghetto, Jacob Gens.

In the Realgymnasium the bonds between young people and teachers were exceptionally strong. Yitskhok wrote to Mani Leyb in 1939 that "we feel totally at home [in our school]". Some of the most poignant passages in Yitskhok's diary describe the emotional shock of the death in the ghetto of a beloved teacher from the Realygymnasium, Yankev Gershteyn, who taught music and directed the choir.

> With what love his beautiful eyes shone hearing a Yiddish word, a Yiddish poem. How much he loved his language, his people. This love, this national pride, which he represented, he tried to kindle in us. We were his disciples. (27 September 1942)

iii

In other parts of Europe there was a long interlude – two or three years – between the arrival of the Germans and the onset of mass murder. But for Yitskhok Rudashevski and the Jews of Vilna, the killing began immediately. They had little chance to escape: German tanks rolled in on 24 June 1941, just two days after the German attack. By the time SS-Einsatzkommando 9 arrived in Vilna, Lithuanian nationalists had already started to kidnap and kill Jewish men. The Lithuanians also told the Germans that they had located a perfect killing site: Ponary, a scenic forest suburb where the Soviets had been digging deep pits to store fuel. By 1944 the forest would contain more than 70,000 bodies.

The Holocaust began in Lithuania. Of the 250,000 Jews in Soviet Lithuania on 22 June 1941, 210,000 were shot that summer and autumn, mainly by Lithuanian collaborators and German Einsatzgruppen. In July the killers murdered mainly men. By August they also began to shoot women and children. Of the 60,000 Jews in Vilna on 22 June, only 18,000 were alive by January. In the summer of 1941, a reign of terror descended on Vilna Jewry: the yellow star, forced labour, large-scale expropriation of Jewish property.

In early September 1941, the Germans forced Jews to leave their homes and enter a ghetto in the rundown streets of the old Jewish quarter in the centre of town. For most Jews the ghetto turned into a death trap as roundups sent thousands of victims to Ponary. The Germans did not forget to couple physical murder with psychological torture. In October they announced that only Jews possessing a "yellow certificate" would remain in the ghetto. They gave the *Judenrat* (Jewish Council) 3000 certificates to distribute. Each holder of a certificate could claim one spouse and two children. It was up to the *Judenrat* to decide who got the certificate, who lived and who died. Twelve thousand Jews would gain the right to stay in the ghetto, the remaining 15,000 were doomed to die – unless they found a good hideout.

Various Jewish institutions received a limited quota of yellow passes, always fewer than the number of employees. It fell to Jewish directors and managers to play God and to decide who would get a pass and who would not. Dr Mark Dvorzhetski, who worked in the Jewish hospital, recalled how he waited alongside a longtime colleague and friend, Dr Kolocner, to learn his fate:

> Both of us sat in the corridor of the Judenrat waiting to learn what would happen. Even as we chatted we knew that a "*shayn*" [certificate] for one of us meant death for the other ... I got the *shayn*, my friend was left to his fate. I was ashamed to look him in the face but I took the document and left. In my place he would have done the same.

When the wave of killing finally subsided in late December, 18,000 Jews were left in the Vilna Ghetto: the 12,000 covered by the certificates and 6000 who crawled out of hideouts after the manhunts ended and whom the Germans eventually allowed to stay.

The "quiet period" of the Vilna Ghetto lasted from January 1942 until April 1943. During these fourteen months Jacob Gens, the controversial Jewish boss of the ghetto, did what he could to buy time, save as many Jews as possible and please the Germans. Unlike most Jews in Vilna, he spoke fluent Lithuanian. A former officer in the Lithuanian army and husband of a Lithuanian woman, Gens made effective use of his contacts with the local Lithuanian collaborators to help the ghetto. He set up workshops, organised schools for the surviving children and smuggled food into the ghetto. Although Jews in the Vilna Ghetto were often hungry, there was little of the mass starvation that decimated the ghettos in Warsaw and Lódź.

In January 1942 Gens suddenly ordered the establishment of a ghetto theatre. Many Jews were shocked. The Germans had just murdered two-thirds of Vilna Jewry, and Gens wanted a theatre! Bundists hung posters warning that "there's no place for a theatre in a cemetery". But Gens insisted and within a few weeks it became clear that the theatre was a success. Tickets quickly sold out. Indeed, no ghetto in Eastern Europe had a more intense and better organised cultural life. First-rate composers, writers, poets and directors – including Wolf Durmashkin, Kasriel Broyde and Leyb Rosenthal – collaborated on a stellar array of original productions as well as high-quality stagings of Jewish classics in Yiddish and Hebrew. There were also art exhibits, a literary society that handed out prizes and encouraged creative writing, a ghetto orchestra and a library that became a focal point of cultural life. As we see from Yitskhok's diary, the ghetto poets Avrom Sutzkever and Shmerke Kaczerginski took the ghetto youth club under their wing.

No one could envy Gens' position or the fraught game that he was trying to play. In his 19 October 1942 diary entry, Yitskhok blasted him and the Jewish police who participated in a selection of more than 400 old and sick Jews whom the Germans soon murdered in the Oszmiana Ghetto. Yitskhok wrote, "The whole ghetto is in an uproar because of this departure. How great is our misfortune, how great is our shame, our humiliation. Jews are helping the Germans in their organised, horrifying extermination."

Yitskhok did not know the back story. Shortly before, the Germans had asked Gens to send Jewish police to carry out a selection in Kiemieliszki. Gens refused and the Germans slaughtered the entire ghetto. Next they asked Gens to send police to Oszmiana for the same job. This time he said yes: he hoped to save the many by sacrificing the few. The Vilna Ghetto police, liberally supplied with alcohol, chose 406 old and sick Jews who had no hope of surviving anyway. When the police returned from Oszmiana, Gens, visibly drunk, called a meeting of the ghetto elite to explain himself:

> I know that a lot of you think I'm a traitor and are asking yourselves, "Why is he here showing his face at this cultural gathering?" I , Gens, lead Jews to their death. I, Gens, rescue Jews from death. I, Gens, destroy hideouts and I, Gens, try to procure more work passes and jobs. My main

concern is Jewish lives, not Jewish honour. When they ask me to hand over a thousand Jews, yes, I hand them over. If I don't the Germans will come into the ghetto, take many thousands and leave the ghetto in shambles … You are the people of art and literature. You people can give the filth in the ghetto a wide berth. And when you leave the ghetto someday, you'll have clean hands and a pure conscience. But if I, Gens, will somehow survive, my hands will be soiled with dripping blood.

The "quiet period" ended on 5 April 1943. After the Germans moved 5000 Jews from surrounding towns into the Vilna Ghetto, which was too crowded to house them, Gens announced that a train would take them to the Kovno Ghetto, where they would work. Gens was so sure the Jews were safe that he offered to travel to Kovno on the same train. But the train took the 5000 Jews to Ponary. Hundreds of Jews attacked the Germans and Lithuanians with knives and fists before they were shot down. Horrified and humiliated, Gens returned to the ghetto. Most of the Jews murdered that day were young and able to work. If the Germans were ready to kill them, what did that mean for Gens' assurances that if the Jews worked hard, the Germans would let them live? That evening Yitskhok wrote:

The ghetto was profoundly shaken, as if struck by a thunderclap. The mood of massacre has taken hold of the population. It has begun again. The claws of the hawk have appeared before us again. People sit confined in a crate and on the other side lurks the enemy, who is preparing to annihilate us in a refined way according to a plan, as today's massacre has shown. The ghetto is dejected and saddened. We are defenceless and faced with death.

Yet even after the April massacre Gens did his best to offer the Jews some shred of hope. If they worked hard and stayed disciplined, they might still have a chance.

Gens' main rival in the ghetto was the FPO (United Partisan Organisation), which was organised in January 1942. On New Year's Eve the poet Abba Kovner had read a proclamation that called on Jews to resist. The murders in Lithuania were no local atrocity but the first act in a German plan to murder all the Jews of Europe. The FPO collected weapons, recruited a few hundred members and prepared to fight the Germans in the ghetto. What mattered for the FPO was to strike a blow for Jewish honour. Sarah Voloshin recalled that the FPO also recruited young people, including Yitskhok and herself, to act as messengers.

The FPO found little support in the ghetto. Jews resented these young people, whom they called "*pishers mit di biksn*", "little squirts with guns", who threated to bring down a calamity on everyone. The showdown between Gens and the FPO took place on 16 July 1943. The Germans demanded that Gens hand over the commander of the FPO, Itzik Vittenberg. As Jewish police led Vittenberg to the ghetto gate, FPO fighters attacked the police and freed him. Gens then told the Jews that the Germans would destroy the ghetto unless they got their hands on Vittenberg. Did they want to die because of one man? As panic-stricken Jews fanned out to hunt for him, the FPO leadership realised that Vittenberg had no choice but to turn himself in. Gens probably slipped him a cyanide pill just before he left the ghetto. The next day the Germans dumped his body at the gate.

The trauma of that day convinced the FPO and its new commander, Abba Kovner, that the fighters had to leave the ghetto for the forests. The Jews of Vilna rejected an armed uprising against the Germans, even after the example of the Warsaw Ghetto Uprising, where the Jews supported the fighters and built 750 bunkers that forced the Germans to spend an entire month clearing the ghetto. The difference between Vilna and Warsaw was that in Warsaw there was no *Judenrat* leader like Gens to convince the Jews that they still had a chance to live.

When the Germans finally liquidated the Vilna Ghetto in September 1943, Gens could have saved himself. His Lithuanian friends offered to hide him. But when Gestapo chief Rudolf

Neugebauer summoned him on 15 September 1943, Gens voluntarily went to his death. He believed that it would be dishonourable to try to save his own life after what had happened to the ghetto. On 23 September a final selection sent most Jews to the gas chambers of Sobibor while the young and healthy went to labour camps in Latvia and Estonia. Of the 60,000 Jews living in Vilna before the war, about 3000 survived.

iv

Yitskhok's diary ends right after the massacre on 5 April 1943. Thus, we do not know how he reacted to the dramatic events during the final period of the ghetto. Did he continue to write? Sarah Voloshin believed that he did not. There is also reason to think, as Voloshin did, that Yitskhok actually began writing the diary in the autumn of 1942 and that the first section, beginning with the outbreak of war in June 1941 – which, unlike the later section, did not include dated entries – was written after the fact. This may also explain the fact that there are minor discrepancies in dates here and there.

How does a fourteen-year-old endure the abrupt end of childhood, the loss of his home, the realisation that his parents can no longer protect him from the worst? The July 1941 decree to wear a yellow patch cut him to the quick. "I felt ashamed … not because I am a Jew but because of what has been done to us. I am ashamed of our helplessness." The move to the ghetto, in the rundown streets and alleys of the old Jewish section, was even more traumatic. On that day, 6 September 1941, long lines of Jews, weighed down by heavy bundles, converged on the ghetto from all directions. They passed through streets lined with jeering Poles and Lithuanians and struggled to keep up the pace. Life or death depended on sheer chance. The Germans arbitrarily diverted some columns that came from northern neighbour-hoods and sent them to their deaths. Jews who trudged in from other directions were allowed to enter. Yitskhok and his family made it into the ghetto, but he could never forget what happened that day, down to the last detail:

> People are harnessed to the bundles they drag along the pavement. People fall. Bundles are scattered. In front of me a woman is bowed under her bundle. From the bundle a thin string of rice pours onto the street. I walk along heavily loaded and wearing multiple layers of clothes. Lithuanians drive us forward, won't let us rest. I do not think about any-thing – not about what I am losing, not about what I have just lost, not about what lies in wait for me … I feel that I have been robbed, that they have robbed me of my freedom, taken me away from my home and away from the familiar Vilna streets that I love so much. Everything is being torn from me.

If some Jews hoped for an end to the roundups once they were in the ghetto, they were badly mistaken. The Germans and Lithuanians mercilessly combed the ghetto and sent Jews without the right papers to Ponary. In October 1941 Yitskhok and his family joined other Jews in a hiding place and had a close call:

My head is spinning, a cold sweat breaks out, my heart stops completely. We are like animals surrounded by hunters. The hunter comes from all directions, under us, above us, on our sides. Broken locks snap, doors scrape, axes and crowbars bang. I feel the enemy under the boards on which I am standing. The light of an electric torch steals through the cracks. They are banging there, smashing, tearing. Soon we hear an attack from another side. Suddenly a child has started to cry. A desperate groan goes out from us all. We are lost. Desperately pushing sugar into the child's mouth doesn't help. It is covered up with pillows. The child's mother cries. People cry in wild terror that the child should be suffocated. The child cries louder. The Lithuanians bang more loudly against the walls. But little by little everything calms down by itself. We understand that they have gone away. Later we hear a voice from outside the *maline*: "You are free." My heart beats with such joy! I have survived!

That day they survived but they knew they were living on borrowed time. Miraculously, just when all seemed lost, Yitskhok's mother managed to procure a coveted yellow certificate. They could now stay in the ghetto. But the family paid a heavy price. They were forced to abandon Yitskhok's beloved grandmother. This was the new reality: each decision was fraught with grave moral consequences. Sarah Voloshin recalled that Yitskhok never got over the loss of his grandmother and missed her terribly, as his diary attests.

> Grandma cannot go with us. We are desperate. In the *maline* in our courtyard they are not letting anyone in. They are already shut tight. What can we do? Meanwhile the stream of people has started to budge and our labour unit is passing through the gate. The stream of people has carried us along. We quickly say goodbye to Grandma – forever. We leave her standing in the middle of the street and run to save ourselves. I will never forget her two pleading hands and eyes which begged us: "Take me with you!"

Once the ghetto "stabilised" in January 1942, Yitskhok's life took a new turn. Since his parents both worked long hours, he was the one who cooked, stood in line for potatoes and scrubbed the floors. The crowded living conditions, the squalor of the tiny ghetto and the injustices that he observed made him deeply angry. In his diary he lambasted the arrogance and brutality of the Jewish police and the gaps between the privileged and the less fortunate. "In the ghetto we see among us Jews so much injustice, so much incorrectness, so much that is disgusting – during the distribution of meat on the ration cards, for example. People freeze while standing in line. Policemen and big shots walk in freely." (5 January 1943)

But he was determined not to give in to despair. He found a new sense of purpose in his schoolwork, his close friends and his club. Given the chance to drop his studies and learn a trade, Yitskhok decided that, come what may, he would continue his education.

> The desire to study has become a kind of defiance of today, a time that detests studying and loves toil and drudgery. No, I decided, I live with tomorrow not with today and if out of a hundred ghetto youth of my age, ten are able to study, I have to be among the lucky ones. (8 January 1943)

Yet again, one sees the degree to which Yiddish literature and culture inspired Yitskhok and his friends in the ghetto. Under the guidance of the poets Sutzkever and Kaczerginski, he helped prepare an exhibit dedicated to the Yiddish poet Yehoash, who translated the Bible into Yiddish. His diary described an evening in memory of the writer Mendele Mocher Sforim. He acted in skits based on the writings of I.L. Peretz and Sholem Aleichem.

Yitskhok and his classmates joined a history circle, led by librarian Herman Kruk, that interviewed Jews in the ghetto about their experiences. He also recorded ghetto folklore: new words, sayings and jokes, how Jews compensated for their power-lessness by making fun of the Germans behind their backs.

Today there is renewed scholarly interest in "Hurbn Yiddish", in what happens to a language whose speakers are suddenly assaulted and murdered. These kids in the Vilna Ghetto already began to ask the right questions.

> In the ghetto, before our own eyes, dozens of sayings, curses, good wishes and terms like *vashenen* – smuggle in – are being created, even songs, jokes and stories that already sound like legends. I feel that I will participate in the circle enthusiasti-cally, because the wonderful ghetto folklore, etched in blood, which abounds in the streets, must be collected and preserved as a treasure for the future. (2 November 1942)

Some of the more problematic passages in Yitskhok's diary are his unstinting praise of Communism, Stalin and the Soviet Union, which controlled Lithuania from 1940 to 1941. In the beginning pages he wrote that "never was life so happy and carefree as in the first Soviet summer of 1941". He recalled how he rushed to meet the Soviet tanks that snuffed out Lithuanian independence in June 1940. Since alleged Jewish collaboration with communists was used to justify collaboration in the killing of Jews, passages such as these could play into the hands of antisemites and apologists for Lithuanian collaboration. And if Yitskhok had wonderful memories of the Soviet summer of 1941, others had different recollections, including the mass arrests carried out by the Soviet secret police just before the German attack in June 1941.

It is all too easy after the fact to criticise the naivety of a fifteen-year-old. By this time he surely knew that the Soviets had murdered many beloved leaders of Jewish Vilna, including Zalmen Reyzen, the editor of the paper that employed Yitskhok's father and uncle, and Anna Rosenthal, the head of the Bund in Vilna. Moyshe Kulbak, one of Vilna's most revered poets, was arrested in Minsk and shot in 1937.

But such questions are beside the point. Every Jew in the Vilna Ghetto knew that the only chance of survival depended on the Red Army. And even if Jews harboured doubts about the Soviet system, there was always hope that things would get better after the war. Yiddishists also remembered that the Soviet Union had offered state support for Yiddish schools and cultural institutions. Yitskhok was still a boy and he followed the lead of adults he respected, like his teacher Mire Bershteyn. Other communists who should have known better, like Shmerke Kaczerginski, only realised their mistake after 1945. Many even kept the faith until years later.

When Avrom Sutzkever first published Yitskhok's diary, in 1953, in his Yiddish literary journal *Di Goldene Keyt*, he carefully excised many of these offending passages.

Years later, the first translations were published by the Ghetto Fighters House (*Beit Lohamei Ha-getaot*), a Hebrew edition in 1968 and an English translation in 1973. In 2016 a French edition was published by Éditions de l'Antilope. None of these translations, however, was completely accurate.

Although the English translation that appeared in 1973 included the sections Sutzkever left out, it was marred by awkward phrasing and, in a few cases, a poor rendering of the original meaning. In terms of syntax and readability, therefore, the present translation by Solon Beinfeld should be considered the standard and authoritative English version of the diary.

For obvious reasons, Yitzhak's pro-Soviet musings seriously complicated efforts to publish the diary in Lithuanian. Having endured decades of Soviet repression, many Lithuanians preferred to remember their own ordeals and forget the widespread collaboration of many of their countrymen in the murder of their Jewish neighbours. Nor could Lithuanians fail to notice that while "good Germans" made cameo appearances in the diary, Lithuanians were invariably portrayed as killers and collaborators.

A complete reckoning with the dark chapters of Lithuanian Jewish relations is still a long way off. But, thanks to scholars such as Mindaugas Kvietkauskas, Lithuanians are getting a more unvarnished view of the Litvak world that was destroyed by the Holocaust. The 2018 publication in Vilnius of a richly illustrated bilingual Yiddish-Lithuanian edition of the Rudashevski diary was a major step forward, as was the decision to teach excerpts from the diary in Lithuanian schools. To be sure, that translation, based on Sutzkever's 1953 publication, is still not a complete version. But its appearance shows that more and more Lithuanians want an honest reckoning with the past.

Yitskhok's last entry was written on 7 April 1943.

The mood has improved a little. In the Club you can already hear a happy little song. But we are prepared for everything, because Monday has revealed that we must trust nobody, believe nobody. At any moment, the worst can happen to us.

It is only right that at last an accurate and complete English version of his diary has appeared, superbly translated by Beinfeld. Hopefully this diary will help readers appreciate just what was lost when the Germans destroyed the Jerusalem of Lithuania, and snuffed out the life of this remarkable fifteen-year-old boy. ≡

Yitskhok Rudashevski with his father, Elihu, in Vilna before the war.
Image courtesy of the US Holocaust Memorial Museum.

The diary of Yitskhok Rudashevski

(translated by Solon Beinfeld)

It is June 1941.

Schoolwork is over. The days are sunny, warm. I feel like getting out of the city. We, the Pioneers, are going to a Pioneer meeting in our schoolyard. We walk along the Vilna streets, which are bathed in sunlight. All we talk about is going to camp. The group dreams of green fields and of cheerful camp life. The group yearns to get out of town.

We travel by steamer to Verek. We are greeted by sunny greenery. In the evening we return to the noisy city that teems with life, with people, with the Red Army men's singing and laughter. Never was life so happy and carefree as in the Soviet summer of 1941.

It is Sunday, 21 June. A beautiful summer day. Our ten-man Pioneer group is scheduled to meet today. I go over to Gabik's house to ask him to notify several friends. I found him busy with his garden bed. Our lively conversation was suddenly interrupted by the howling of a siren. The siren seemed out of place in the midst of the peaceful summer spread out around us. The siren cruelly cut through the blue air, portending something cruel. The evening of this beautiful summer day was disturbed. Bombs burst all over the city. The street was full of smoke. It is war. People ran around in confusion. Everything has suddenly changed so much. The peaceful blue sky has turned into a volcano that pelts the stunned city with bombs. It became clear to everyone: the Nazis have attacked our land, they have forced a war upon us. Well, we will fight back and fight on until we have beaten the attacker on his own soil. I look at the calm Red Army man standing guard in our courtyard. I feel secure with him. He will not disappear. He may be killed, but the star on his cap has risen and will endure forever.

We are sitting in a cellar. The roar of the propellers outside does not allow us to think, then suddenly – a whistle and a bang, then a second, a third, coming down like hail. Things calm down. I think about our life in the future. I think that we Pioneers, too, will not shy away from the battle. I feel that we will be found useful. We will receive our assignments.

Soon we need to go to our club. At six o'clock a meeting of our Pioneer group was supposed to take place. I decide that we must go. I feel that we Pioneers now understand that we will have certain responsibilities in the future. The struggle is beginning. The Soviet land will rise up. With these thoughts I go to our meeting place in the little garden area on Railway Street. I carry with me *The Hero in Chains* [*Les Misérables*], from which we will read together about Gavroche, the child of the Paris proletariat who fell on the barricades alongside the adult fighters. I come to the woody lot. Nobody is there. But, after a while, Serke arrives. We talk about the latest events. We were soon terrified by the first German bombs. Of all the comrades, just two came and that is because we live near the railway. Now, as I write, I think that we have become quite different Pioneers. I feel that when we are needed, we will come, even if it is the last Pioneer gathering.

Serke and I sit for a while in the garden. The bombing has ceased, as if the weather had cleared up. But suddenly – the siren again. We run home. Explosions rattle the air again. There is banging and howling outside. In the cellar in front of me I see frightened people, with bundles. No one knows what awaits us. The gloomy evening arrives. Full of fear, people await the oncoming night. I go out into the street. Trucks keep driving past. The black sky is lit with red. Somewhere a big fire is burning.

Monday was restless as well. Red Army soldiers, crowded into trucks, roll endlessly towards Lipuvke. The population is fleeing too. People say, with desperation, that the Red Army is abandoning us. The Germans are approaching Vilna. The evening of that desperate day arrives. I see trucks with Red Army men fleeing. I understand, they are leaving us. But I am sure that resistance will come. I watch the fleeing army and I am sure that it will return with victory.

The night is uneasy. The trucks roar in the street. From time to time shooting starts up. A neighbour notices a red star in my lapel. He tells me that it must be removed. I cannot make peace with the idea. Is it really like that already? I am filled with resentment and pain that it should end this way. But I sense that he is right.

It is Tuesday, 24 June [actually 23 June 1941]. I observe the empty, sad streets. A Lithuanian with a gun is standing in the street. I begin to grasp the vile treason of the Lithuanians: they shot the Red Army men in the back. They are going along with the Nazi bandits. The Red Army will return and you will pay dearly, traitor! We will outlive you – that is our answer to the Lithuanian soldier with the Haenel gun. A motorcycle drives through the early morning street: a grey, angular helmet, glasses, an overcoat and a gun. Unfortunately, I have spotted the first soldier of the German army of occupation. His helmet flashes evil and cold. A little while later I go out into the street. Today at ten o'clock we were supposed to have a gathering of our ten-man Pioneer group. Today the school library is open. I know that I will find no one there. I go there anyway. It has all happened too quickly, too suddenly. It is hard to grasp that everything has truly been interrupted. I reach the doorstep – the school is sealed shut. I meet a friend. Like strangers we walk the wide streets. The German army is on the move. The two of us stand with downcast eyes. A black apparition of tanks, motorcycles, cars. I recall how almost exactly a year ago I welcomed the Red Army in a little Lithuanian town. We ran for several kilometres to greet the first Soviet tank that had stopped there. A year has passed since then and now German tanks are riding through the streets of Vilna. And it seems to me like it's some unfortunate mistake that will soon be corrected. I imagine life under the

I look at the triumphant advance of the Germans and am already thinking of their retreat

Germans as brief and temporary. I look at the triumphant advance of the Germans and am already thinking of their retreat. I imagine them fleeing to the rear, battered and overwhelmed.

I went to see my teacher Mire. She was sitting there depressed. We understood one another. She told us to make sure our Pioneer neckties are well hidden. I went to see my friend Benye Nayer. I found him heating the stove with magazines, books, notebooks. When I came home, I too heated the stove and stashed away the necktie. The first day under the German occupation has passed. I lie at night and think. German trucks keep rolling, by day and by night. I think how helpless we are, separated from one another, exposed to the mercy of the Nazis.

Weeks go by. I am cut off from the summer, from my surroundings, chained to the house, to the courtyard. I don't see any of my friends. There is no contact at all among the group. Everyone is preoccupied with his own day-to-day worries. Jews are humiliated and exploited.

We have to stand in long lines to obtain bread and other foodstuffs. Jews are pushed out of them. Germans come up to the queues and throw the Jews out. Jews receive less food than the Aryans. Our life is a life of helpless fear. Our day is without a future. There is one consolation. The Red Army has pulled itself together. It gives back a blow for every blow. It is putting up a resistance. The Germans have realised they are not going to get this done in no time. They are dealing with a brave fighter who will not leave us in the lurch.

Lithuanian "catchers" go through the houses, grab Jewish men. They gather them up in groups and hustle them off to work. Many do not return. I sometimes go to the courtyard of the Jewish community building at 6 Strashun Street. I bring my father food there. Many Jews have been assembled there. From there they are taken to work. I go into the courtyard. The courtyard is filled with a herd of men, grey, gloomy, helpless men, like a big, frightened, murmuring herd. From time to time a woman runs into the courtyard, weeping. Everyone comes here with his misfortunes, to the little room where the first *Judenrat* [Jewish Council] sits. Each one thinks, or wants to think, that this is where he will be helped. Soon a German bursts into the courtyard. People rush over to him and importune him, because he is known to be a good German. The German picks out a group of healthy men, chooses them like horses, looking at their muscles, then lines them up and tells them to go. The others start to follow as well. The German drives them away with his belt …

It is evening. "We've made it through another day," the wives say to one another. The men of our courtyard arrive, sweaty and covered with dust. All day long they carry boxes in the weapons storehouses.

It is heartbreaking to see the shameful scenes of Jewish women and old people being beaten and kicked in the middle of the street by young hooligans. It is a performance. Germans stand and look on. A throng of Gentile women gathers. I stand at the window and feel a seething sensation in me. My eyes fill with tears. Our whole helplessness, our whole wretchedness, lies out there in the streets. There is no one to defend us and we ourselves are so helpless, so helpless! Life becomes harder and harder. We do not go anywhere. In dozens of streets a Jew dare not show himself. Only in the morning do the frightened Jewish women slip out to buy something. The men leave for work. It rains and rains without stopping. It is all so sad. We are so alone. We are exposed to mockery and humiliation. Every now and then a new fear grips several tenants in our courtyard. They are being searched for weapons. The courtyard is full of Germans. The bell rings at the door, the door is torn open and everyone's heart is pounding. Germans in helmets barge in, their weapons clanging. The closets and drawers are opened for them obediently. They brutally toss everything apart. They fling and throw, then go away, leaving behind them a sad home with clothes strewn all over. We all stand pale-faced. We calm down only when we have found out that they are gone. The mood grows worse from day to day. There is talk of a ghetto. On rainy evenings we meet at a neighbour's house and talk about the news, about the ghetto question, which has now become timely.

One evening, two Germans came into the courtyard on motorcycles and went upstairs to a neighbour. They came from Glubok.

[Friday, 5 September 1941] On 8 July the decree is issued that the Vilna Jewish population must put on a yellow patch front and back, a circle with a J in it. It is dawn. I look out of the window and I see the first Vilna Jews with patches. It pains me to see how people are staring at them. The big pieces of yellow material on their backs burn inside me. For a long time, I couldn't put on the patches. It felt like a hump and two frogs were on me. I felt ashamed to appear with them in the street, not because I am a Jew, but because I am ashamed of what has been done to us. I was ashamed of our helplessness ... They will hang patches on us from head to toe and we can do nothing about it. It pained me that I could see no way out. Now we pay no attention to the patches. The patch sits on our coats, but it has not touched our sense of who we are. We now have so much awareness of who we are that we can say that we feel no shame with the patches! Let those who hung them on us feel shame. Let them burn inside every conscious German who tries to ponder the future of his people.

It is the end of the summer of 1941. We do not know what awaits us. I have never felt the arrival of autumn as much as I do now. The days become more and more anxious. Jewish furniture is confiscated. There is talk of a ghetto. Suddenly the terrifying news spreads about the provocation on Daytshe, Shavler, Mikolayever, Disner and other narrow streets. At night the Jewish population of those streets was taken away. No one knows where to. Later it became known that it was to Ponar, where they were executed by shooting. The situation has become more and more tense. The Jews in our courtyard are desperate. They take their possessions to their Christian neighbours. The sad days of tying up bundles have begun, of sleepless nights full of anxiously awaiting the coming day. It is the night of the 5th of September, a sleepless, beautiful September night. A sleepless, despairing night. People, like shadows, sit helplessly with their bundles, painfully waiting. Tomorrow we will be led into the ghetto.

[Saturday, 6 September 1941] It is the 6th of September. It dawned a beautiful, sunny day. The streets are cordoned off by Lithuanians. There is an anxious feeling. Jewish workers are allowed through. A ghetto is being created for the Jews of Vilna.

At home we are packing. The women go around wringing their hands, weeping as they see their homes looking like after a pogrom. I walk around, weary from lack of sleep, among the bundles. I see how overnight we are uprooted from our homes. Soon we get a glimpse of the first image of going to the ghetto. It is an image from the Middle Ages. A big black mass of people moves, harnessed to their big bundles. We understand that it will soon be our turn. I look at the disorderly room, at the bundles, at the overwhelmed, despairing people. I see things lying around that had become so dear to me, which I used to use. Soon, two Christian neighbours [arrive to look at our room]. We carry the bundles into the courtyard. On our street a new mass of Jews keeps streaming to the ghetto. The small number of Jews in our courtyard begin to drag their bundles to the gate. Christians stand nearby and look on. Some Jews hire Christian boys to help them carry the bundles. A package was suddenly stolen from a neighbour. The woman stands in distress among her bundles. She has no idea what to do. She weeps and wrings her hands. Suddenly weeping fills the air, everyone is weeping. People cry looking at the bundles they do not know what to do with. One woman's bundle has split open. Eggs begin to scatter ... The sun, as if ashamed of what people are doing down below, lets the sky cloud over. It begins to rain. We too are carried along with the stream of Jews with bundles. Shavler Street is streaming with Jews with bundles, moving slowly. It is the first great tragedy. People are harnessed to the bundles they drag along the pavement. People fall. Bundles are scattered. In front of me a woman is bowed under her bundle. From the bundle a thin string of rice pours onto the street. I walk along heavily loaded and wearing multiple layers of clothes. Lithuanians drive us forward, won't let us rest. I do not think about anything – not about what I am losing, not about what I have just lost, not about what lies in wait for me. I do not see the street or the passers-by. I feel only that I am exhausted. A feeling of being insulted and a pain burn inside me. I feel like crying. It is the ghetto gate already. I feel that I have been robbed, that they have robbed me of my freedom, taken me away from my home and away from the familiar Vilna streets that I love so much. Everything is being torn from me. At the gate there is a crush of people. At last I am on the other side of the [ghetto] gate. The stream of people shoves me into a gate flooded with parcels. I throw off the bundles, which are cutting into my shoulders. I locate my parents and here we are in our ghetto home. It is evening, very dark and rainy. The little streets Rudnitsker, Shavler, Yatkever, Shpitol [Hospital] Street, Disner, which make up the ghetto, look like anthills. They teem with people. Those who have arrived begin to settle in, each in his own little bit of space. Additional Jews keep streaming in without interruption. We settle into our space. In addition to the four of us, there are eleven people in the room. The room is dirty and muddy. It is cramped. The first ghetto night. Three of us lie on two doors. I do not sleep. My ears are filled with the lamentation of this day. I hear the uneasy breathing of the people with whom I have so suddenly been thrown together, people who have suddenly been uprooted from their homes just like me.

[September 1941?] The first ghetto day dawns. I run straight out into the street. The streets are still filled with a restless mass of people. It is hard to push your way through. I feel like I am in a chest. There is no air to breathe. Wherever you go you run into a gate that cuts us off from Strashun Street. That is part of the ghetto too. I look for relatives and friends. Some people still have no place to live. They settle in on stairs and in shops. Suddenly the mass of people in the street starts to sway. People start to run. German officers are coming to photograph the crooked alleys, the frightened people. They are satisfied with the Middle Ages which they have brought all the way to the twentieth century!!! Soon they leave. People calm down. I decide I have to find my friends. I think we have to be together. Soon I find Benke Nayer, Gabik and several others. The first day in the ghetto is taken up with settling in, searching for one another. The second evening in the ghetto people feel a little bit more at home, calmer. My group of friends is already calculating how many weeks we shall have to stay here. At night things are disturbed again. German soldiers sneaked into the ghetto to rob. They knock on gates. People hurriedly get dressed in the crowded space and then three soldiers rush in, crawl over the bedding with their feet, look for rings on people's fingers, ransack and make a mess of the room where people are sleeping. They leave, taking nothing. The women shout after them, "Thank you, dear sir, good night." Is the idea that you should thank them because they have not robbed you? At a time when the robber does not even want to hear? I am disgusted with you, I am enraged. The exasperated people wish each other a good, calm night and lie down again.

[Wednesday, 1 October 1941] The first ghetto days pass by. Father goes to work again in the munition storehouses. In the house it is cramped and smoky. I go, like many others, to hunt for wood. We break up doors and floors and carry off the wood. One person tries to snatch from another. People fight over a piece of wood. We already see the first effect our condition has on people. People become petty, egoistic and even cruel to one another. Soon we see the first Jewish policemen. They are supposed to maintain order in the ghetto. In time, they become a caste that helps the oppressors do their work. Over time, many things were done by the Gestapo with the help of the Jewish police. They help grab their brother by the throat; they help trip up their brother.

In the evening the Jews come back from work exhausted, depressed. I go to meet my father. At the ghetto gate the group forms itself into a single line. Then the arriving workers are let through. The little sacks of potatoes and flour that they have managed to buy in town are confiscated from them.

I often go with my father to his workplace. I see the Vilna streets. The unit goes to the Burbishok armament storehouses. The road there is beautiful. The storehouses are located in a beautiful, fenced wood. It is fresh and pleasant there. I breathe more easily. Soon the men turn to the gear and boxes in the warehouse. In the evening, I go back with the unit and hurry back into the ghetto.

In the morning a lot of people go out, as if they were Christians, to their Christian neighbours to reclaim clothing, food. In the morning I too went out and soon returned with a full knapsack. Two weeks of ghetto life have gone by. The workers at the most important German labour units get a skilled-worker stamp on their labour certificates. Those who receive a certificate like that are forced to go over, with their families, to the second ghetto. The life that had just become settled is shaken once again. Once again, anxious people, burdened with bundles, move to the second ghetto.

Today is Yom Kippur. I am not well. I have a fever. Today the ghetto is full of storm troopers. They thought today Jews would not be going to work so they have come to take them. At night things suddenly become restless. People get up. The gate is opened.

Everyone looks for a place to conceal himself, to save his life

There is a commotion. Lithuanians have arrived. I look out at the courtyard. I see that people with bundles are already being taken away. I hear boots stomping on the stairs. Soon, however, things calm down. The Lithuanians are given money and leave. That is the way in which the defenceless Jews attempt to save themselves.

In the morning the terrible news spreads around. Overnight, several thousand people were dragged out of the ghetto. These people never came back. Later we learn about the liquidation of the second ghetto. The same thing happened there as with us and is continuing. Anxious, turbulent days have arrived. People of the other ghetto saved themselves by running to this ghetto. Thus, the second ghetto became a trap to ensnare thousands of defenceless Jews. In our ghetto things are very troubled. The white certificates are replaced by yellow ones, very few of which are issued. Thus was born the yellow certificate, the bloody illusion which was such a tragedy for the Jews of Vilna. The days are filled with anticipation – days before a storm. People, helpless creatures, stagger around the little streets like animals that sense a storm. Everyone looks for a place to conceal himself, to save his life. They register themselves as relatives of those who have a yellow certificate. Fate has suddenly split the people of the ghetto into two parts. One part possesses the yellow certificate. They believe in the power of this piece of paper. It gives you the right to life. The other half – lost, helpless people who sense their downfall and do not know where to turn.

We do not have a yellow certificate. My parents, like hundreds of others, are running around feverishly. Something horrible is hanging in the air. Soon, soon, something will burst. A troubled evening arrives. The little streets are full of people. Those with yellow certificates are being registered. Whoever can do so hides himself! The word *maline* has become current. Hide yourself, bury yourself in a cellar, in an attic. Save yourself. Dozens of people plead with those standing in line, the chosen ones, to inscribe them onto their yellow certificates. For inscribing they offer gold, money.

Our neighbours in the house go into a *maline*. We go with them, into a three-storey small warehouse at 4 Shavler Street. There are steps between the levels. The stairs between the first and second levels have been removed. The entrance has been boarded up. The *maline* consists of two storage levels. In the middle there is a hole in the wall of a dwelling that is adjacent to the upper storey of the *maline*. The hole is cleverly concealed by a kitchen cabinet. One wall of the cabinet is, at the same time, a door for the hole. The hole is barricaded with stones. The dwelling through which you enter the *maline* is located next to our flat. Small groups of people with packages go in there. Soon we crawl through the hole of the *maline* as well. A lot of people have gathered in the two levels of the *maline*. They shuffle along by candlelight like ghosts along the cold, bare cellar walls. The whole *maline* is filled with anxious murmuring. A mass of imprisoned people. Each person begins to settle into his little corner, or on the stairs. People place pillows, bundles on the hard bricks and boards, and fall asleep. The candles begin to go out and everything is wrapped in darkness. All you hear is the snoring of the sleepers, the sighing and restless murmuring. There's not enough air to breathe. The odour of a cellar, of people squeezed together. From time to time someone lights a match. By its light

I see people lying like rags in dirt, on the bricks. I think about what a helpless, broken creature man can turn into. I don't know what to do with myself. I start to feel nauseous. I barely make it to dawn. The people crawl out. Dawn brings new news. The yellow-certificate holders and their families will have to leave the ghetto. They will leave and now the game will begin. I look at the mass of people with their bundles streaming towards the gate. They are going to life. I envy them so much. I too would now like to be leaving the accursed ghetto, which is becoming a terrible trap. I wish I were going away, like them, the yellow-certificate people, leaving the storm behind me. Saving my life. I encounter my friend Benye Nayer. He is pale, did not get much sleep. He spent the night in a *maline* too. That is the last time that I saw him. We are mostly in the *maline*. We anticipate something at any moment. Lying there on bundles I fell asleep. I had a terrible dream. I was awakened by a noise and by people pushing against each other. I understood – the Lithuanians are already in the ghetto. The *maline* becomes more and more packed. At the end we are so packed together that it is impossible to move. The *maline* is boarded up. My parents are somewhere upstairs. I am below with my uncle. The *maline* is filled with anxious whispering. Candles are lit and people reassure one another. Suddenly something like steps. People press closer together. An old man was left hanging in the narrow passage from the first to the second level. His feet are moving over the heads of the people below. He is brought down. People call out for water. But gradually everything calms down and everything becomes hushed and enveloped in a black, terrifying silence, a silence from which the tragedy of our helplessness cries out. We sense what is happening outside. A destructive storm is now moving over the ghetto. We hear a kind of distant sound, like a storm being interrupted by cries and shots. My heart beats as if being hammered to the beat of the storm outside. I soon feel that the storm is growing closer to us. My head is spinning, a cold sweat breaks out, my heart stops completely. We are like animals surrounded by hunters. The hunter comes from all directions, under us, above us, on our sides. Broken locks snap, doors scrape, axes and crowbars bang. I feel the enemy under the boards on which I am standing. The light of an electric torch steals through the cracks. They are banging there, smashing, tearing. Soon we hear an attack from another side. Suddenly a child has started to cry. A desperate groan goes out from us all. We are lost. Desperately pushing sugar into the child's mouth doesn't help. It is covered up with pillows. The child's mother cries. People cry in wild terror that the child should be suffocated. The child cries louder. The Lithuanians bang more loudly against the walls. But little by little everything calms down by itself. We understand that they have gone away. Later we hear a voice from outside the *maline*:

"You are free." My heart beats with such joy! I have survived!

Saving your own life at all costs, even at the price of our brothers who are departing. Saving your own life and not trying to defend yourself. Such is the point of view of our dying passively, like sheep, unconscious of our tragic fragmentation, our helplessness.

We creep out of the *maline* after our six-hour imprisonment. It is eight o'clock in the evening. Everything resembles the aftermath of a catastrophe. Clothing is scattered around the courtyard. Broken-off locks lie underfoot. Everything is overturned, broken. All the doors are wide open. The house is unrecognisable. It is a ruin. Everything scattered about, many things broken. A bottle of alcohol lies smashed in the middle of the room. The bundles are ripped open with knives. I go out into the street. It is dark, filled with the silence and with the tragedy that has just happened here. Packages lie on the pavement, a bloody reminder of the people who have just been wrenched away to their deaths. I go into the courtyard where my cousins live. I spot two big lighted windows. I look inside. A room like after a pogrom. The electric light is on, but there are no people to be seen. It is so terrible. I stand all alone in the big courtyard. I go into my uncle's house. It is dark, I step on things. It is quiet. A clock ticks alone like an orphan. There is no one there.

I go back home. Frightened people crawl out of corners. They too have been saved.

In the middle of the night the holders of the yellow certificates begin to return. How dreadful it is at daybreak. About 5000 people were wrenched away last night. They were taken off to the Lukishki Prison. The ghetto is full of weeping and of lamenting, shattered people. This one is searching for a father, this one a mother, this one a child. Families were divided. One went out to be saved, the second was torn away. I run to Benye Nayer's. He is not there! So many young lives have been cut short. I have lost such a good friend. I constantly think about this dear fellow. We miss him now, Benye Nayer. In the ghetto he often thought about where we stand now. He said he would not go to Ponar. But it seems that he too went away. I will always remember you, Benye! We will avenge you. In the street I run into Gabik. We went off to our teacher Mire. Here too there is a fresh wound. Teacher Mire's parents have been taken away.

My uncle and my cousins have come from a *maline*. They jumped over rooftops. They were fired at. They escaped into the attic of a Christian house and saved themselves. They are completely covered in coal dust. That is how people are starting to find each other. We constantly learn of new misfortunes.

Several days have passed. The wound is still bleeding. Part of those taken away were led to the second ghetto, but most of them to Lukishki and from there to Ponar. Ponar – that word is written in blood. Ponar – the huge grave. The green area up the Pohulanke road, a slaughterhouse for thousands of Jews. The Ponar area is saturated with Jewish blood. Ponar is the same thing as a nightmare, a nightmare that has accompanied the grey thread of our ghetto days. Ponar is passive death. The word contains the tragedy of our helplessness. No! We will not go to Ponar.

We live in the ghetto as possessors of white certificates. The mood of slaughter has not yet disappeared. What has happened will soon be repeated. In the meantime, life is so hard. The holders of white certificates do not go out to work. Everything is very expensive in the ghetto. In the evening I walk around in the ghetto. From the gate the yellow-certificate holders arrive with bundles. I look at them with envy. Suddenly there is a commotion. The cry: "We want to eat too!" is heard. People yell and tear the bundles away from the arrivals. I see a man with hungry eyes cut open a bag of potatoes on someone's back. Potatoes scatter around the street! "We want to eat too ..." A commotion follows. Policemen beat and drive people away. At night we sleep mostly in the *maline*. I really wish I could get undressed and lie down in a bed. In the *maline* there is a cold, hard floor to lie on. Mice squeak all around. There are big shots in the *maline* who sleep in their own clean little storerooms.

[January/February 1942?] Mother went out with a labour unit. Maybe she will be able to get a yellow certificate there. Meanwhile, in the evening, an order was issued that all persons with white certificates must immediately move into the second ghetto, which has been designated for them. Now our street, Shavler, has to assemble. We feel that we dare not go to the second ghetto. Meanwhile we pack our bundles again. The bundles become fewer and fewer through all these commotions. Our courtyard is full of people with bundles. The policemen urge them to move faster. The frightened people sense that they should not go. I have already felt the cunning of the exterminators. But the Jewish police stand at the side and assure them that they ought to go, because Murer [the assistant in charge of Jewish affairs for Vilna's Nazi government] has promised that there will be a ghetto with a Jewish council there. The mass of people believe the Jewish police and go ahead blindly. We go with our bundles, but I call out to my father that we should force our way through the policemen over to Shpitol Street, because mother will not know where we are. We force our way to acquaintances who live on Shpitol Street. My uncle went away to the second ghetto. In the evening mother comes back empty-handed. We are anxious; we have slept badly. We don't know what to do next. The other people in the room hold yellow certificates. I look with envy at their calmness, their assurance that they will live. There is a policeman living in the room as well. He boasts that the Jewish police managed in three hours' time to transfer about 600 families. Murer is satisfied. As a result, the ghetto is secure.

In the morning, people again headed for the second ghetto. Mother went off to her labour unit. During the day the movement to the second ghetto was halted. In that ghetto the game began. Again, the second ghetto became a trap for the blind mass of Jews. I can't forget about my uncle, who went away there. We were together the whole time and all of a sudden we are separated. We went off to the right – he to the left, into the trap. In the evening mother comes back, again empty-handed. She tells us that the *aktsye* [operation] within the ghetto is going on without interruption.

The next morning I saw Kasrilke Krause's brother. He is the only one left. His mother, sister and Kasrilke went away to the second ghetto. He has remained all alone. He doesn't know what to do. He has no possessions, no money. All day long I wait for my mother. She has brought a yellow certificate that gives us the right to life. I too have gone over to the more or less calm group – the holders of yellow certificates.

People are fleeing the ghetto.

We have received a note from the uncle in the second ghetto. They are in a *maline* there. The liquidation of that ghetto is going on without interruption. Every day you see little groups of people with small bundles who are running away from the ghetto. They run wherever their eyes and legs carry them – to White Russia [Belarus], to the villages, to Christians, to try to save themselves.

In the ghetto things have become very restless. The yellow-certificate holders have received the order to leave the ghetto with their families. Soon the little ghetto streets are deserted. People scatter to *malines*. We take small bundles and join the stream of the chosen who are leaving the ghetto. Our cousins who have been inscribed with us come along. It is a cloudy, muddy day. A wet snow is falling. It will take a long time till we reach the gate because the inspection there is very thorough. All around us there is weeping. People are saying goodbye to their close kin who are staying behind here in the ghetto in *malines*. We learn that old people who are written down as parents are not allowed to pass through the gate. Grandma cannot go with us. We are desperate. In the *maline* in our courtyard they are not letting anyone in. They are already shut tight. What can we do? Meanwhile the stream of people has started to budge and our labour unit is passing through the gate. The stream of people has carried us along. We quickly say goodbye to Grandma – forever. We leave her standing in the middle of the street and run to save ourselves. I will never forget her two pleading hands and eyes which begged us: "Take me with you!" We leave the ghetto which has been left vacant so that soon the savage Lithuanians can break into the defenceless little streets. We go to the gate as a mass of selected people, squeezed together, fleeing the ghetto, leaving their nearest and dearest abandoned. German officers stand on both sides of the pavement. They hurry and push us forward. At the barrier there is an inspection. Older people are flung into the nearby guardhouse. We push our way through. Our certificates are inspected. The Lithuanian officers are herding people to the gate, their rubber nightsticks raised. They drive the select few to life ... Now we are already on the street. We can see the executioners. My heart is beating. Lithuanian detachments are encircling the ghetto. Soon, soon, they will be crawling inside.

They let us go where we want – either to the labour unit workplaces or to the second ghetto. The streets fill with small groups of Jews, like flocks that have lost their way. We walk in the middle of the street. Trucks speed by and splatter us with mud. Mother and I go to her workplace, the *Schneiderstube* [tailoring workshop]. We sat there the whole day. As I sit, I look at the well-fed, satisfied Germans who come and go, at the tormented Jewish workers who are awaiting the relatives they have left in the ghetto. They offer money to the German policemen to go and pluck out of the ghetto the brothers, sisters and parents the workers have left behind.

In the evening we go to the second ghetto. We meet with my uncle. For over a week he has been sitting in a *maline* in the second ghetto, in a tiny room concealed by an armoire. We lie on our bundles in the room where my uncle lives. We are broken and exhausted. Mother is crying. We cannot forget leaving Grandma behind. Sick at heart, we lie down to sleep in the new location.

The narrow streets of the second ghetto are full of people. They tell about the latest news from the first ghetto, that many *malines* were discovered, hundreds of people from that ghetto were dragged away to Lukishki Prison. Vayskop, the head of the *Schneiderstube*, is doing a lot of business in the meantime. For a lot of money, he goes with the German police to take people out of the [Lukishki] Prison. I walk around the narrow streets of the second ghetto, the alleys of the old ghetto of Vilna. Never has so much ruin and desolation descended on them as now. The old *Shulhoyf* [courtyard of the Great Synagogue] looks like after a pogrom. Phylacteries, religious books, loose pages of sacred texts lie underfoot. Everything in the second ghetto is destroyed, broken, abandoned. The lamentation of those who were torn away from here pervades everything. The word Ponar hovers over all the ghetto streets. After spending three days in the second ghetto, we return to the gate of ghetto number one. There is no inspection to get into the ghetto. In the ghetto it is devastation. Doors overturned, floors torn up. We enter our room. Everything is broken and ripped apart. People come out from the *malines* like cadavers, pale, filthy with black circles under their eyes. People have lain for three days stuffed into holes and cellars. Grandma is not here. The room is filled with weeping and cries. I flee from the house. I walk around the streets. In me, pain and resentment are burning. I feel that we are like sheep. They slaughter us in the thousands. We are helpless. The enemy is strong and cunning. He is killing us off with a plan and we are powerless.

Jews must live in housing blocks with the labour units where they work. We have moved into the block as well.

Life has gradually begun to become "normalised". The handful of remaining Jews are starting to get used to the new conditions. My parents are working and I have become the "housewife" in the flat. I have learned to cook, wash the floors, and that is how my days go by. In the evening I go to meet my parents. Groups of Jewish workers come from town in miserable condition. A grey mass keeps streaming through the gate, free labour for the profiteers. It is forbidden to bring in food from town through the gate. The Jewish workers find a solution by carrying the food under their clothes. At the gate they are patted down and the little bits of property are taken away. This honourable work is carried out by the Jewish police.

Winter is drawing near, bringing new everyday worries: warm clothes, wood. Along with winter a new certificate has emerged – the pink family certificate, issued to family members of yellow-certificate holders. The situation becomes anxious again. At the end of December there is a new *aktsye* [Ger. *Aktion* – here, an anti-Jewish operation] that snatches away a couple of hundred new people. It is a frosty day. We are not allowed to walk in the streets. Lithuanians go through the houses and take away whoever does not have a pink certificate. We sit at home and see through the window as they lead people to their deaths.

After that, things calm down again. A hard winter has set in. Before dawn I go out to stand in line. It is still dark outside. The little streets are in the grip of the frost. It's still before dawn and you already see a long line of people standing next to the walls.

These days I occupy myself with keeping house. In the evening I go out to meet my parents. It's already dark. The Jewish workers arrive, covered in snow and freezing. The lantern sways sadly above the ghetto gate, lighting the falling snowflakes and the Lithuanian in his fur coat who is inspecting the Jewish workers. I walk around the ghetto streets. People walk quickly; it's cold. "A candle, a candle, whom can I sell light to?" A little boy runs down the street trembling with cold. How much sadness the ghetto day contains within itself. I do not see any friends. The grey everyday routine has separated us. The only consolation has become the latest news from the front. Here we are suffering, but there, far to the east, things have picked up. The Red Army has begun an offensive. The Soviets have captured Rostov, delivered a blow from within Moscow, and are moving forward. It always seems to me that any minute now freedom will return.

Monday, 23 March [1942] All of a sudden – a series of loud banging noises. It lasts several hours. I am in the cellar of the courtyard. I hear the explosions and I realise that those are our Soviet flyers. For several hours they delivered bombs, then left. In the city they created destruction in the Lithuanian barracks. They let them know that they are strong and are on their way. How horrible the little ghetto streets look under a cloudy sky that is lit up every now and then into a dazzling shade of red.

Saturday, 12 [September 1942]. Today is a holiday, the Jewish New Year *Rosheshone*. The day is cooler than the days have been lately. The sky is clear. In the morning I went down into the street. A solemnity that is far from joyousness is spread over the few little ghetto streets. It all feels empty. It reminds me somewhat of earlier times. A voice praying out loud can be heard coming from somewhere. Here and there women go by with holiday kerchiefs on their heads and with holiday prayer books under their arms. I was reminded of my grandmother. She too went to the synagogue like that once a year. Near the ghetto guardhouse, on the hated ghetto gate, there hangs a big sign: a *Leshone toyve*. The gate watch is wishing us a good year ... These holiday greetings, on a gate lined with barbed wire, signed by the gate watchmen, made a strange impression on me. They are wishing us a good year against the backdrop of the ghetto gate that expresses the darkness and desolation of ghetto life. And who is wishing it for us? Those who, though not of their own free will, were nevertheless organised to keep watch on us and keep us far away from freedom. But still, let us assume that through that same gate we will return to freedom.

It is evening. I go out into the street. The streets are lively. People walk around dressed up. It's a holiday. It is noticeable in every home you enter – the poverty has been cleaned up. But now I feel strangely good, because the daily grey days badly need a little bit of a holiday to chase away, for a while, the grey of the everyday. People walk around the little Vilna ghetto streets until late. The mood is a strangely sad holiday mood. Now the crowd is getting sparser and sparser. The cold is nipping at us. A cold starry sky. From time to time a falling star streaks across the sky with its silvery trail, until it falls down.

Sunday, 13 [September 1942]. The fourth number of the *Geto-yedies* [*Ghetto News*] has appeared, a holiday issue. In the first place they wish a happy new year to our dear [ghetto chief] Gens and all those others. An interview with Gens is quite interesting. Winter is coming on and the ghetto is concerned about housing and clothing. Gens also talks about the past of the ghetto. The most painful part of it is, of course, missing. You cannot ask questions about it and you will receive no answers. Until spring, the ghetto was typified by chaos. Now in the ghetto we have made it our goal to assemble all of its labour force, because it is only thanks to our labour that we exist. Starting in the spring, intensive ghetto labour has been taking place in the ghetto itself. Many enterprises have been opened and completed. Our Commander hopes, and is certain, that we will live to see happier times.

At home today we had a few good laughs. The workers in our flat are from the famous *Schneiderstube*. Mother works there too. They talk about their whole week, how Jewish tailors get along with the Germans and get some provisions from them. The workers talk about life there. It's drudgery, but at the same time they need to chase after a piece of bread, make a living. They buy and sell, trade with a peasant, make a deal using an old piece of clothing. But all that is only until a German appears and then they run off at once. But they are not so impressed by the Germans. If they catch a simpleton of a *yeke* [German, pejorative] who wants a cap, the group pull his leg. They present him with a Jew who they say is "the best capmaker in Poland". The German believes them. Then they tell him that this diligent Jew can only make beautiful caps if he gets some food. He is persuaded and it arrives. He takes out material that would suffice for three hats, but they tell him that this is nothing much. When it comes time to receive it, he is simply told: "Listen, do you have cigarettes? Give us cigarettes and you will have '*eine entzückende Mütze*' ['a delightful cap']." At the end they make a hat that looks like a *blintz* on him and on top of that he exclaims, "Jews are a capable people." We wish him "*mitn rosh in [der] adome"* [Yiddish, using Hebrew nouns: "with your head in the ground"] and he answers, "Many thanks." They call out after him, *"A nomen nokh dir,"* [literally, "named after you" when you have died] and he is delighted with his "cap". That is how our tailors work. The workers say it sometimes looks like a Jewish bazaar. With the Germans they get along pretty well. "Yankl," yells one tailor to another, "take this *Herr* to be measured for *tachrichim* [shrouds], or this one, if you please, to the *taare-bret* [board for purification of the bodies of the dead], quick!" Or "make a nice *rekele* [diminutive of *rak*, cancer] for the side of this German lady [supposedly meaning – sew a jacket (*rok*, diminutive *rekele*) for her]". The Jewish female embroiderers make monograms, in which the ornament consists of four Jewish letters: *giml – a gzeyre* [persecution], *tsadek – a tsore* [affliction], *samech – a sreyfe* [conflagration], *kof – a kapore* [expiatory sacrifice]. All these acts are thumbing your nose, covered up. In reality, they live in fear of the Germans. Still, they allow themselves to curse, to play a trick. They do it, though, only when it is possible.

Monday, 14 [September 1942]. Today we learned that school has been postponed again for a week. Many teachers have gone away for work in the countryside. It's a great pity. I long for the studies which keep us going in the ghetto. Without them we become lazier and more careless.

Wednesday, 16 [September 1942]. I have a bit of a cold, a catarrh. I sit at home. In the street it's drizzling. It's lonesome, there's nothing to do. The rainy, cold autumn has arrived.

Thursday, 17 September [1942]. It's getting colder and colder. How dreary and gloomy the ghetto appears. A cold rain whips across the little crooked streets. It gets sad and boring during the long hours when you hang around in one place. We don't go to school because of an epidemic. It's a terrible time when you can't pull yourself together to do some work and you waste whole days doing nothing. In the evening, when people return from work, they seat themselves closely together and talk about the news: political news and ghetto news. They tell that here and there people have secretly listened to the radio and things like that. Summer is over. During the summer people were expecting German successes. The war in the east has, up to now, in the year 1942, been divided into two main parts: winter and spring, when we were all hoping for a great Soviet winter offensive. The Soviets accomplished a great deal during the winter just by putting the invading German army on the defensive, driving it out of many positions. The winter revealed a lot to us but did not decide anything. In the summer the German offensive began. The German attack in the south has been successful. In the centre and north the Soviets continue to attack without interruption and have seized the initiative. In the south, where the Germans have hurled tremendous forces, they have occupied all of Crimea, capturing the Soviet base, the port of Sevastopol. The Soviet attack at Kharkov also failed. The Germans have had successes in Ukraine. They have penetrated very deep, with the aim of cutting off the centre of the Caucasus. German army units, capturing Lugansk, Novorossiysk and other cities, have advanced as far as the Caucasus Mountains. It is impossible to go any further. The Germans are now mounting a huge attack on Stalingrad (Tsaritsyn). Stalingrad has tremendous importance for both sides. By capturing Stalingrad, the Germans would be cutting off the centre of the Caucasus. By capturing Stalingrad, the Germans would reach the Volga,

Everyone is waiting for the longed-for peace when the exhausted world will straighten its back

seizing its largest and most important port. At a time when in the central and northern front the Soviets have the total initiative – at Voronezh, Rzhev – and when south of [Lake] Ladoga and across the Neva near Leningrad a huge Soviet attack is taking place, at Stalingrad the Soviets need to be on the defensive. At Stalingrad, battles of tremendous scope are now taking place. Both opponents have concentrated their strongest forces there. In addition to its strategic importance, Stalingrad has become a matter of prestige for both sides. The Germans want to conclude their summer campaign by capturing Stalingrad, which would crown the German victories. The Red Army is battling in the suburbs of Stalingrad with great stubbornness and heroism. Tens of thousands of men perish in the giant battles at Stalingrad. The Soviet people are defending Stalin's city with all their might. We, sitting in the ghetto, read the reports every day and run around looking for good news. Everyone's attention is now turned to Stalingrad. Everyone is waiting, exhausted, for something concrete, for Germany's decisive defeat. Everyone is waiting for the longed-for peace when the exhausted world will straighten its back.

Friday, 18 September [1942]. In the evening we learn of a meeting of the brigadiers. Brigadiers are a sort of caste in the ghetto, a class. The Jews work outside the ghetto in a variety of German and municipal labour units, in columns. For every column, there is a column leader or brigadier. When there is news, or orders from the authorities, Gens assembles the brigadiers. By nightfall, we have already found out the news from the meeting. The group of brigadiers assemble in the ghetto theatre. This time the speaker was Levas, the Commander of the Gate Guard. Naturally, he spoke about his own affairs. He informs them that starting today, and for the time being, all bringing in of things must stop. He announces that the fate of the ghetto depends on the gate. Levas states that the ghetto inhabitants and the police will have to show ingenuity to see to it that nothing is brought in and yet everything is available in the ghetto. "Therefore," Levas concludes, "I order that in the upcoming days nothing is to be brought in, reception hours starting at nine in the evening." That last bit he repeated three times. The ghetto inhabitant doesn't need it to be repeated many times. They understand it perfectly well. That is, at nine o'clock even oxen could be brought in. In general, everything in the ghetto depends on the gate. When no foodstuffs are allowed in, there is scarcity. Let the Jewish police allow bringing in for just an hour, then the ghetto will be full of food. In the ghetto you can get everything in great quantities. But everything is terribly expensive and only a small percentage can afford to live like in the past. A greater part of the ghetto lives modestly and by far the greatest part suffers from hunger. That is the tragic picture that the ghetto represents. A brother is forced to beat a brother and take away from him the hard-earned piece of bread that he brings in for his family.

Saturday, 19 September [1942]. It's cold and melancholy. Will I ever live to see my studies begin? When I used to go to school I knew how to divide my day and the days flew by. Now they are grey and sad. Oh, how sad and lonesome it is to sit locked away in a ghetto …

Sunday, 20 [September 1942]. It is Yom Kippur eve. Sad feelings hover over the ghetto. It is such a sad holiday. Before the ghetto, and even now, I am very far from religion, but still I feel it deep in my heart, this ghetto celebration of a holiday drenched [last year] in blood and sorrow. This evening was so sad for me. We sit in the house and people cry. They recall the past. They kiss each other and exchange wishes, greeting each other with tears. I run out into the street. There it is the same thing: sorrow hovers over the little streets, the ghetto is steeped in tears. The ghetto inmates, whose hearts have been hardened by the knot of ghetto worries and who have had no time to cry their hearts out, now in this evening of weeping have poured out all their bitterness. For me it has been a sad, dark and sorrowful evening.

Monday, 21 [September 1942]. The holiday is evident in the ghetto. It is quiet. It is a sunny and cold day. Here and there an old Jewish man goes by with a *tallis*, pushing a handcart full of bricks into the "liberated territories". (The City Hall has awarded to the ghetto an additional stretch of Yatkever Street and the Oshmener Alley. In the evening I go out with some friends through the dark little streets.) "It was just such a night," one of them says. Yes, a year ago at this time, it was the terrible night of Yom Kippur. It grows dark. The moon, round and dull, wanders between the little black clouds, illuminating the spires of the church that overlooks the ghetto across the crooked black roofs. We are overcome by a feeling of dread. "It was dark, the streets were full of indistinct murmuring. In the dark, people were being herded like sheep, their rolls of bed-linen shimmering white. People were driven forward with bayonets. People were walking and groping in the dark. Old Jewish men groaned: 'We can't see where to go.' And at midnight the iron gate of the prison closed behind us." Late, after the curfew whistle, we go off to our homes.

Thursday, 24 September [1942]. For several days I haven't felt well. From time to time I have a fever. I have a bad taste in my mouth. I can't eat. I feel cold. There's no limit to my tedium and boredom. Much of the day I lie in bed. It will probably pass. Luckily, I have an extraordinary book, Kellermann's *The Ninth of November*. This book has made a strong impression on me. The book is a description of the previous world war. We see the whole horror of war, which puts such a dark imprint on human life. The ninth of November, that is the day when the German people, the exhausted front soldiers, raised the red flag of freedom, the people's wrath spilling over into the famished streets. Ackermann, the hero of the book, the front soldier with three wounds in his broad, unbuttoned coat – how beautiful, how idealistic is this image of the soldier in the light of the revolution.

Sunday, 27 [September 1942]. Today I woke up with a very high fever. I feel very unwell. I have a temperature of 39 degrees. How awful it is to be sick in the ghetto, in a cramped, stuffy room, among the packages. It's been a week since I began feeling unwell and today I finally can't get up. All along I didn't want to get up, because I understood what a treat it is to lie down in our "palace", where people are stifled and rub up against each other in a small room. The doctor who came over found that I had a light case of jaundice. He prescribed several medications and a diet. In the evening, lying in bed with a high temperature, I learned of the great misfortune. Our dear, beloved Gershteyn has died. Like a thunderclap I was struck by the painful news – Teacher Gershteyn is dead. How dear and beloved to me was his pure and proud figure. And now, lying in bed, I sense the tremendous loss. How could we imagine our beloved school, which stood firmly over the years and educated a new generation, without Teacher Gershteyn? How much Teacher Gershteyn was loved in school. How everyone who knew him loved this handsome, tall figure who looked so fine against the backdrop of our *gimnazye*. How youthfully he would climb the stairs at school, galoshes in hand and with a cane. How majestically he would stride down the school corridors, through the auditorium. If a picture of a Yiddish writer wasn't hung totally straight, Teacher Gershteyn was there and with what love he straightened out the picture.

With what love his beautiful eyes shone hearing a Yiddish word, a Yiddish poem. How much he loved his language, his people. This love, this national pride, which he represented, he tried to kindle in us. We were his disciples. When Gershteyn would enter his class, the mood became altogether different. How pleasing was his pure, lionlike voice, which would warmly and cordially call out: "Good morning to you, children. I have new merchandise for you (he would hand out *Grininke Beymelekh* [*Little Green Trees*], *Khaver* [*Comrade*] and *Kinder-fraynd* [*Children's Friend*]), hand over your coins!" He would take out his big bag, take the money and distribute the fresh magazines. His eyes glowed with kindness and devotion. What beautiful songs Gershteyn sang with us. His favourite song was:

> I have seen Yiddish words
> Like glimmering flames,
> Like beautiful flames.
> I have seen Yiddish words
> Like little small doves,
> Like cooing small doves.

Gershteyn's chorus was the jewel of our school. And he was beloved not only in the school. The public loved Gershteyn's chorus. I remember that before the Soviets came, we started getting letters from a cousin of mine from the distant Urals, from Sverdlovsk. In the first letter she asked about Gershteyn – how is his chorus doing? (My cousin had sung in Gershteyn's chorus.) With most people's lives so grey and ordinary, Gershteyn represented for everybody a kind of unique beauty. Gershteyn was a person of a generous nature and of wide knowledge. In addition to his deep understanding of his people and language, Gershteyn also embodied the universal.

But all that we previously had has been cut off from us. The ghetto has been a tragedy for Jewish Vilna. In the ghetto died Teacher Gershon Pludermakher, the Teacher [Malke] Khayimson-Bastomski and Teacher Gershteyn. Three old teachers, three old oaks rooted in Jewish Vilna and who lit up her name. Teacher Gershteyn suffered a great deal in the ghetto. He grew greyer and greyer, his face grew dark. He lived in a classroom of our *gimnazye*. He could barely go up the steps he used to climb in such a lively way. He had to pause at every step, in his wrinkled coat which undoubtedly served him as a pillow. I remember a rainy day when I saw Gershteyn near the door of the school. He asked me to go up and ask his sister for his galoshes. It was hard for him to go back up the stairs. Slowly, old before his time, he would walk the streets of the ghetto, but with his head held high, as always. Yes, that is how our best people suffered in the ghetto. Last winter, together with several other boys, I carried Gershteyn's possessions over to a new dwelling. We spoke with him. That is how he lived in the ghetto, quiet in his suffering, together with his sister. (Two of his sisters were taken away.) Gershteyn also taught in the ghetto middle school. Until the last moment he did not forget his duty. The ghetto was too hard for Gershteyn and he was not able to hold out. I thought about Teacher Gershteyn for a very long time. I see him before my eyes. He appears before me, so handsome, so fresh, amid the grey, dreary life all around. Always, always, we will remember you as a dear friend. The image of your proud figure will always remind us that you gave us something dear and beloved. And your name will always remain alive among us.

Monday, 28 [September 1942]. Today I feel better. My temperature has gone down. Today at half past four Gershteyn's funeral took place. He lay there all day, I am told by friends who came to see me, with his beautiful head on a pressed white pillow, uncovered and surrounded by flowers ... I was very sorry I couldn't be present at his funeral. Thousands of people accompanied him. The crowd of students, teachers, friends and ordinary workers streamed, filled with anger. Up to the hated gate came the furious crowd. The crowd did not rage openly, but everyone was raging inwardly ... And I, lying in bed, also raged when in my thoughts I accompanied Gershteyn and felt myself also going to the gate and being driven back. At that point, like hundreds of Jews, I felt fury in me. But times will change. With songs and flowers we will march to the tombs of our heroes.

Tuesday, 29 [September 1942]. My temperature has already gone down. But I'm still lying in bed. The whites of my eyes are yellow, but the doctor says it will soon pass.

Wednesday, 30 [September 1942]. I'm already out of bed. I feel good, but there's one misfortune. I have become really famished. I'm not supposed to eat bread, eggs, meat and butter. I have become weak and I desperately want to eat. That is a good sign ...

Friday, 2 [October 1942]. I am by now almost well. I walk around in the street. Since new streets have been added to our ghetto which border on our Disner Alley and since our alley is bordered by ruins that stretch all the way across Yatkever Street, they are being torn down. All day long they bang with hammers. They toss a rope around a piece of ruin and with a bang like a bomb, a piece of ruin comes down. Now just walls of demolished stone buildings are standing.

By daylight you can see the blue sky, and at night the stars, through the holes that once were windows. Strange feelings envelop me. Looking at the black ruins, I recall the bloody storms that used to sweep over our ghetto. I look into the black hole, at the remnants of stoves. How much tragedy and pain are reflected in every smashed brick, every black crack, every flake of plaster and every strip of wallpaper. Here the murderers, the Lithuanians, broke their way in with axes and crowbars, looking for their prey: women, children, men ... Through here, hungry people would crawl out of the ghetto to bring in something to eat. Here in these ruins, like furious beasts hunting their prey, people broke and pierced the walls, ripping out boards with which to cook their wretched meals. Not far from this ruin and another one, Jewish lawbreakers were hanged while Germans stood there laughing at the horror ... And Jews walked around the ruins, biting their lips till they bled, out of pain and shame ... Here, here, here on the black

It seems to me that the ruins weep and cry out as if lives were concealed within

walls, is written in blood and tears the whole of our tragedy and pain. I get an odd feeling looking at the ruins as Jews rummage around. I too crawl though the bricks, bits of wallpaper and tiles, and it seems to me that a lamentation echoes from the black cracks and gaping holes. It seems to me that the ruins weep and cry out as if lives were concealed within ... I recall Bialik's lines: "And crawl through attics and through dwellings full of holes and take a deep look into all the black holes. They are open, mute wounds and they no longer wait for a remedy in the world." It horrifies me how, like a ghost in the ghetto, the naked wall stands and importunes and haunts and opens everyone's wounds ... Everyone is glad as it crashes down and grows smaller and smaller.

Sunday, 4 [October 1942]. In the evening, in the hall of the former Jewish bank, there took place a memorial service on the occasion of the death of Gershteyn, organised by the *Beutelager* labour unit and its brigadier, Kaplan-Kaplanski. A big audience gathers. Among flowers and lighting, you see Gershteyn's two last portraits, drawn by the artist Rokhl Sutskever: Gershteyn on his death bed. The memorial service made a great impression on me. Kaplan-Kaplanski speaks about Gershteyn, as the great humanitarian and as the proud Jew. In his words, he brings to life much of the past: the *Vilner Tog* newspaper and the other institutions around which Jewish Vilna was concentrated and where Gershteyn was everywhere in the forefront. Teacher Lubotski also speaks about Gershteyn. By their words they awaken in us an even deeper love for the deceased. All the numbers of the memorial are impressive and powerful. Standing, we listen to a funeral march. The mood is painful and sad. A large audience of workers and children, mixed together, stands while the sad notes play. Several poems are recited.

A violinist performs several pieces dedicated to Gershteyn's passing – touching, mournful tones, full of frustration, pain and love for the deceased. The tones pour forth and I look closely at the death portrait. He looks as if he were sleeping, lulled by the melody played for him ... Lyuba Levitska sings several songs that Gershteyn loved and used to sing with his chorus. The poet Sutskever reads a poem on the occasion of Gershteyn's death. He writes that "human feelings are now like candles without a wick and melt into themselves ..." But Gershteyn's death has struck something, as if a wall had fallen on you. We wanted to believe that you would survive, you "proudest of men ..." If this were a different time, we would be carrying "his flower-body to sow it", but now we cannot even accompany him ... We turn back and "breathe his anger ..." Yes, the audience disperses and breathes Gershteyn's anger, which dominates us.

Monday, 5 [October 1942]. I made it there at last! Today we are going to school. This was an altogether different day. Courses, subjects. Both sixth grades have been combined. In school the mood is happy. Finally, the Club has opened as well. My life is settling in quite differently! Far less time is being wasted. My day is organised and passes quickly, quickly ... Yes, that's what we need in the ghetto – that the day should pass quickly and time should not be wasted.

Wednesday, 7 [October 1942]. Life has become a little more interesting. Work at the Club has begun. We have literary and natural science circles. When I leave class at 7.30 I go straight to the Club. There the mood is cheerful. We enjoy ourselves and in a big group we go home in the evening. The days are short and it is dark in the street. The bunch of us leaves the Club making noise and a commotion. The police yell at us, but we do not listen to them.

Friday, 9 [October 1942]. Today I had a difficult day. I washed the floor, chopped wood, aired the bedclothes and cooked. It was very hard for me. All sweaty, I ran around the whole day and wore myself out. I was almost unable to study. At night I did not feel well. It turns out I caught a cold. At night I had a high fever.

Saturday, 10 [October 1942]. I have had a high fever all day long. I feel very unwell. The doctor says I have a very bad cold. At night I sweated a lot. Everything I had on was soaked.

Sunday, 11 [October 1942]. Today I feel much better. I have read *Three of Them* by Gorki. The book made a strong impression on me.

Monday, 12 [October 1942]. My temperature has fallen. I read, I write.

Tuesday, 13 [October 1942]. I'm out of bed. I don't go out into the street. You have to be careful not to catch cold.

Wednesday, 14 [October 1942]. Today I spent all day writing an essay on *The Ninth of November*, a book that has captivated me. I copied out many splendid excerpts – powerful, everlasting words which announce the freedom of all nations.

Thursday, 15 [October 1942]. Today I went to school. In the streets it is rainy and gloomy. It's cold in the street, so I won't go out today. I am reading Bergelson's *Penek*.

Saturday, 17 [October 1942]. A boring day. My mood is the same as the weather outside. I ask myself: what would it be like if we didn't go to school, to the Club and didn't read any books? We would undoubtedly die of unhappiness within the walls of the ghetto. There is no school today. On the other hand, things liven up when people return from work. People tell the news – naturally the good news. The Soviets have crossed the Don. People get excited and argue. We are told that the Germans have been unable to take Stalingrad. They are standing still. "That's why they have confiscated all the chairs in the ghetto – they're tired of standing there, so they want to sit down for a while," someone chimes in. I go out into the street. There's a commotion near a bakery. A woman grabbed a pot from the bakery and ran away. People chased and beat her. This brought out feelings of disgust in me. It's terrible, saddening – people are tearing bits of food from each other's mouths. I am filled with pity for the hungry woman, how she is being insulted with the filthiest words, how she is being beaten. I think: what strangely ugly things take place in the ghetto. On the one hand the ugliness of stealing a pot of food, on the other hand the crudeness of beating a woman in the face because she is probably hungry.

Sunday, 18 [October 1942]. A historic day in the ghetto. People are moving into the added "territories", Oshmener Alley. We can now move freely in the new courtyards. A rainy, cold day. I am filled with a strange, sad feeling. On this rainy, muddy day, people are moving in with bundles. Something comes to mind. Ghetto, rainy day, bundles – that is something I already have felt deep in my heart. The ghetto is agitated. I walk around looking at the new "territories", and while doing this I get a pleasant feeling, crawling over the several new courtyards, seeing new places, the big brick ghetto wall, only just constructed. This is the simple feeling of a prisoner who has found a new bit of space in his cell. He looks it over and for the moment he is pleased. Something new in his cell life. But soon I sense another feeling, one of hostility. Hostile to me is the disgusting garbage, the little courtyards, the little street. Cold filth confronts you from every corner. Many houses are shattered, in ruins. At a time when our ghetto streets are painfully engraved in my heart and are familiar and even dear to me because they are saturated with the blood and tears of my brothers, the added courtyards seem cold and unfriendly to me. All day long I crawl around among the courtyards. Just now I see the free world: the church near the barracks on Lidske Street, the bombed-out black, rain-soaked ruins now in their place. Nevertheless, I feel today a little bit as if we had gone out from the ghetto. People now walk, they stream. I don't feel any joy, but I do feel the pleasure of taking a step behind the old gate, to spite that wooden fence with the barbed wire. I make a first round of the ghetto, another one and a third and I soon sense that it is the same prison, only a little bigger, as if they were teasing us. The feeling I had of being about to leave the ghetto vanishes. On the contrary, I feel bitterness.

The old gate is being torn down. The boards and barbed wire are getting tangled up under the blows of the axes and roll up so that it all looks like a spider. After the demolition of the gate at Yatkever Street, the ruins of Yatkever and Disner streets look exposed and naked, with nothing to hold on to. For a long time I continue to walk around in our new spaces. The empty dwellings, the ruins, the abandoned cellars, evoke in me an unpleasant feeling and my mood grows worse and worse, just like the weather, which becomes drearier and muddier. The rain bothers me. It is cold. The wind whistles through the ruins. The whole ghetto seems to be swimming in sombre muddiness. In the evening there is a new sensation. Jewish policemen have suddenly, out of nowhere, put on military caps. I cross the street and here come some of them in leather jackets, boots and round green caps with glossy visors and stars of David. There goes Smilgovski (an "officer") in a navy-blue cap with a gold star of David. With great fanfare they all march together in step (their jackets borrowed by force on the streets). They make the same impression as the Lithuanians, as the "catchers". I am overcome with an unpleasant feeling. I hate them with all my heart, these ghetto Jews in formation. How proudly they strut in their stolen boots! The whole ghetto is in an agitated state. Everyone in the ghetto feels that way about them. They have become so alien to the ghetto. They provoke in me a mixed feeling of derision, disgust and fear. They say in the ghetto that the reason for the uniforms is that thirty Vilna Ghetto policemen are going to nearby towns in order to establish a ghetto in Oshmene. It is not known for certain.

Monday, 19 [October 1942]. The news has spread like a whirlwind through the ghetto. Today thirty Jewish policemen are leaving for the small towns for a certain assignment on the orders of the Gestapo. The ghetto is in mourning. Humiliation and misfortune have attained their highest level. Jews will dip their hands into the very dirtiest and bloodiest activity. Simply put, they will replace the Lithuanians. Our Jewish policemen are now travelling to Oshmene. They are taking along certificates. They will transfer the Jews from the nearby small towns to Oshmene and there *aktsyes* will take place, the same tragic and bloody story as in Vilna. And there our policemen will be the most active participants in all of it. I stand at the gate. They drive me away, but I see everything. Thirty policemen, one and all dressed in leather coats and the new green caps, arranged in two rows, and a certain Weiss, the dog from the Gestapo, commands them. Now they climb into a closed truck. All dressed up, they will

How great is our misfortune, how great is our shame, our humiliation

come to those wretched people. There the Gestapo men will be killing two birds with one stone: first they will accomplish yet another bloody piece of work – certificates, ghettos, packing bundles. We victims understand what that involves. Second, they will demonstrate that uniformed Jews drive their own brothers into ghettos, pass out certificates and maintain order with whips. They say that they went off with thousands in cash. Vilna people who have relatives in those small towns have already paid large sums so that their relatives should get certificates, because we Vilna residents already know that a certificate is a life-saver. The whole ghetto is in an uproar because of this departure. How great is our misfortune, how great is our shame, our humiliation. Jews are helping the Germans in their organised, horrifying extermination.

Tuesday [20 October 1942]. Today we had a meeting of the natural science circle. Teacher Movshovitsh gave a lecture entitled "The Exploitation of Nature for Mankind". It was very interesting. Man utilises nature in various ways. Making use of nature provides mankind with an easier, more comfortable life and people can develop along with civilisation. But with civilisation comes war. Mankind experiences a painful tragedy. The pluses and minuses are in conflict. With life's embellishment comes its annihilation.

Wednesday [21 October 1942]. Today in the Club we did a review of the artistic strengths of the Club: recitation of texts and dance, which we can perform at any time. The Club is preparing an appearance before the workers of the *Beutelager* labour unit. All the numbers were presented before a jury commission. Until eleven o'clock we sat and heard them out. Splendid songs, bright young voices. Beautifully recited was Gorki's poem "The [Song of the] Stormy Petrel", as were the poem "*Hent*" ["Hands"] and the poem "Vilna". The poems were all so sincere, intimate and powerful that our hearts were deeply touched. Some people read their own writings aloud. Particularly beautiful was Yankelev's poem "The Night and the Lightning". The lightning cuts through the night and reveals a hidden sun. Late at night I go home. The rain-soaked streets are wet and empty. I go around armed with the password. The password is "Carmen". It is pleasant to walk quickly, quickly, through the empty little streets and pound loudly with my feet. I call out the password to the three policemen. They sing me back the password from the gate and I am already home.

Thursday, 22 [October 1942]. The days go by quickly. I did my various assignments, occupied myself a bit with housekeeping. Read a short book, wrote in my diary and off to class. The classes went by fast: Latin, mathematics, history, Yiddish, then back home, had a bite to eat and off to the Club. Here we enjoy ourselves a bit. Today there was an inspection led by Yashunski (the head of the Education Department). We also watched the Club's *Maydim* (puppets) performed by two boys. It's quite good, though pretty primitive. The literary side is very weak, but it doesn't matter if we see creativity. Our youth is at work and is not going under. Our history circle is functioning. We hear lectures about the great French Revolution and its phases. The second branch of the history circle – ghetto history – is also at work.

We are researching the courtyard at 4 Shavler Street. For that purpose questionnaires, with the questions to be posed to the ghetto inhabitants, have been distributed among the members. We have already begun the work. I go with a friend. The questions are divided into four periods: questions dealing with the Poles, the Soviets, the Germans (before the ghetto) and in the ghetto. The inhabitants answer in different ways, but everywhere it is the same tragic ghetto-refrain – possessions, certificates, *malines*, loss of property, loss of loved ones. I have tasted the work of the historian. I sit at the table and ask questions and write down the immense griefs drily, factually. I write, I immerse myself in details and do not realise that I am immersing myself in wounds. And what answers people casually give me: They took away two sons and a husband. The sons on Monday, the husband Thursday. And this horror, this tragedy, is formulated by me in three words, coldly and drily. I ponder this and the words look up at me with flame and blood ...

Sunday, 25 [October 1942]. People are moving out of our room. My uncle and his family, who have been living together with us, were notified that they have been assigned a room in the newly added courtyards. A restless day – our little room is in a disorderly state. But nevertheless I'm pleased. It had become impossible to live in such cramped quarters, one on top of the other. We lived four people in a room of 9 square metres. And in this little room there's also a big wardrobe and a divan. After school we went to the meeting of the *Beutelager*. It is an outstanding labour unit. Its brigadier, Kaplan-Kaplanski, organises a meeting of the workers every Sunday. The meeting is of a cultural nature. At today's meeting, Yashunski, the head of the Education Department in the ghetto, reported on the work of the department. In the ghetto right now there are already functioning three elementary schools with three kindergartens, a technical school, a music school, a high school, a children's home and an orphanage for abandoned youth. Each of these institutions has behind it a rich history of martyrdom. Yashunski also spoke about theatre and sport in the ghetto. The second half of the meeting was devoted to appearances by members of the Club, presenting the best numbers chosen at our review. The meetings of the *Beutelager* make a very good impression. How pleasant it is to spend several hours in a cultural environment. Kaplan-Kaplanski thanked Yashunski for his report, but he also made several demands of him: in the ghetto there are people of culture going around without work. He also demands, in the name of the community as a whole, work for Zalmen Reyzen's wife, for Gershteyn's sister and for Teacher Anilovitsh. Kaplan-Kaplanski donated fifty salvaged books to the ghetto library. We sit in the ghetto like convicts in a prison, but we do not let our spirits droop. Jewish workers met and enjoyed two hours spent in a cultural environment that recalled the good, sweet times.

At night I walk around the new ghetto streets. It is a bright night, with a full, round moon. Its laughing, human face stays up in the sky and pours its icy-cold light onto the little streets. The little windows of the buildings are black. From each of them emanate the grey everyday worries, the everyday uneasiness. It is quiet. From somewhere far off you hear the long, drawn-out whistle of a departing train. It pierces the night with sadness and calls out and haunts.

Monday, 26 [October 1942]. Today my father stayed home. We cleaned up. As a result of the moving, things were in disorder and we straightened them up. In the room it's a lot more spacious and comfortable. In school we had a Gershteyn commemoration. Teacher Lubotski told us about our great friend and educator. Students also read their compositions. I also read my composition, "Teacher Gershteyn Has Died".

Tuesday, 27 [October 1942]. Life has become much easier. It is comfortable and quiet in the room. I am the master here myself. I put things in order, clean up and then do my homework. I am busy with going to the apartments on 4 Shavler Street with the questionnaire for research about the ghetto. I am reading, in Polish, *Yellow Cross* by Andrzej Strug. It's a good book, a picture of World War I. There is a lot which is comparable to our war, the same bloodbath, the same tragedy. In school I found out that since my essay for the Gershteyn commemoration was very well written, Teacher Lubotski proposed that I should read it at the memorial in the ghetto theatre this evening at 8.30. I was pretty unprepared – this was unexpected. I arrived half an hour early. I rehearsed reading. As usual, I was nervous. The hall was packed with people. Teacher Lubotski went with me into the wings. With a pounding heart I experienced the day's performance of Slyep's Chorus. They splendidly sang the song:

Sing the lovely Yiddish sounds, Oh chorus,
For the Western sky is red.
Though no sun now shines before us,
Though the poet now is dead.

In the wings, things are interesting as well. The speakers are preparing themselves, talking among themselves and I among them. It turns out, unexpectedly, that I have been asked to sit at the speakers' table. That seems strange to me. The artists and speakers make room for me and decide with me the order of the speakers. My cheeks are burning ... Finally, we are all sitting at the table on the stage: Lubotski, Opeskin, Blyakher, Rubina and Rotnberg. At the beginning I feel uncomfortable. But the wide-ranging, excellent speeches and the love shown for Gershteyn, that beautiful figure, calm me down. The speakers speak at length. Whole eras and times of Gershteyn's beautiful life are evoked. Finally, Teacher Lubotski finishes. He ends by saying that we do not know what life will be like after the war. But we do know one thing: that Gershteyn's place is empty and there is no one to replace him. In the period when we will be rebuilding, we will recognise how great was our loss. Finally, I read my essay. The nervousness I have felt up to now disappears. I feel quite free. I make an effort to read in a loud voice, with expression. The moments fly by like arrows from a bow. "Teacher Gershteyn is for me forever unique, beautiful and joyous." And finally I read the end: "The name Yankev Gershteyn will forever remain among us as a reminder of what is dearest and best." I take my seat. I feel I am blushing again. I felt so uplifted while reading. As I was reading, I felt Teacher Gershteyn deep in my heart. At night a group of us return home. They tell me I read well, a good piece of work. As I lie in bed, my cheeks are still burning ... I will never forget the whole evening, being seated at the speakers' table, my reading, just as I will never forget Teacher Gershteyn.

Friday, 30 October [1942]. Today was a day of work. Until now I had seldom done the cooking. My parents eat a meal at work, and they bring food for me as well. I busied myself with cooking a cabbage and on the second burner, meatballs with potatoes. I worked hard on all that. The room became messy. It is hard to do everything at once. In the meantime, there was turmoil in the ghetto. What it's about, nobody knows. We are not allowed to go out into the street. The Jewish policemen run through the courtyards like wild animals, urge the housecleaners to start sweeping and run upstairs to announce in the rooms that they are to clean up quickly. Finally, the meal is finished. There will be enough for tomorrow too. As if in a fog, I absent-mindedly clean and sweep. Now everything is all cleaned up. I eat something and catch my breath. It turns out that they are expecting "distinguished guests", supposedly some sort of committee from Berlin. The mind of the ghetto is distracted, "it's not itself". That doesn't bother me. I am used to these panic attacks. In the evening we have a meeting of the nature circle. The topic is "Colours in Nature". The nature circle meetings are very interesting. In general, it is interesting in the ghetto to read about, and be involved with, nature. It shows that we are not cut off from nature in the ghetto. We feel it and have a healthy understanding of it.

Saturday, 31 [October 1942]. Finally, some sort of commission arrived in the ghetto. The streets were closed off. Evidently, they didn't enjoy spending time here and they left. In the evening, our neighbour, who works with my parents, brought home a Soviet leaflet. There was a holiday atmosphere in the house. Someone sits at the table and reads aloud. Everyone around him sits open-mouthed and with bated breath. What a treasure, one that comes from far, far away, over battlefields and cities and finally over the barbed wire of the ghetto gate. "*News of the Soviet Fatherland. Death to the German Occupiers.*" Everyone looks at the little piece of paper. It is for each of us such a rarity, such an occasion for celebration. In the leaflet it says we should not believe the German communiqués. The flyer encourages the brothers and sisters of the temporarily occupied regions. The leaflet is dated 11 August. In the communiqué from the front there is nothing particularly important. The Kuban Cossack Division commanded by Tutarinov has distinguished itself in the Caucasus. Likewise, at Briansk, the Soviet tank columns defeated the enemy.

The leaflet talks about life in the Soviet Union. It is so wonderful for me to hear that life is still going on somewhere. The Russian nation is breathing, living and fighting. In the Soviet Union a great social challenge is taking place on a gigantic scale in all sectors. The outstanding factories and labour units in the production of tanks and planes and in the extraction of petroleum are listed. The culture of the present time is written about. The education of children is still at the same high level; tens of thousands of the children of front soldiers are being maintained in children's homes. Recently two films were produced which depict the great struggle: *The Rai-Kom Commissar* and *Partisans*. The leaflet tells about the preparation in England for a second front. The workers of England and America are demanding of their governments that they deliver the decisive battle against Hitlerism. The leaflet describes the glorious work of the Russian partisans. The leaflet ends with a call to the men and women of the partisan movement to carry out sabotage, to derail the German trains! The neighbour let me keep the proclamation. I look at the modest piece of paper; it seems to me that all the exertions and self-sacrifice of the Russian people are embodied in it. I run to the Club with the leaflet to show it to my friends. I keep it in my inside pocket. It seems to me that the letters warm me. The words feel so close, so friendly. We stand in the corners of the Club and read. Everyone felt joyful and in good spirits for a while – we have received greetings from our liberators.

Sunday, 1 November [1942]. It is a beautiful day today. Day in, day out, it's cloudy, rainy. Today it's as if a spring day had arisen between the autumn days. The sky is blue, the sun warms us pleasantly, so the ghetto population flooded the streets to catch what are probably the very last rays of the sun. Our policemen have dressed up in their new hats. Here one of them goes by.

My blood boils. He's in a leather coat, his head held arrogantly high, with his officer's cap askew. The visor gleams in the sun. The strap is tucked under his chin. He struts with his shiny boots. Well fed, stuffed, he conducts himself in the manner of an officer. The scoundrel enjoys that kind of life and acts out his comedy. That is the reason for all my anger at them – in their own tragedy, they play a comedy.

Monday, 2 November [1942]. Today our circle had a very interesting meeting with the poet A. Sutskever. He spoke to us about poetry, about the art of poetry in general and about the varieties of poetry. At the meeting, two important and interesting things were decided. We are creating the following branches of our literary circle: Yiddish poetry and, most important, a group to concern itself with ghetto folklore. I was very interested in, and attracted to, this circle. We have already discussed certain details. In the ghetto, before our own eyes, dozens of sayings, curses, good wishes and terms like *vashenen* – smuggle in – are being created, even songs, jokes and stories that already sound like legends. I feel that I will participate in the circle enthusiastically, because the wonderful ghetto folklore, etched in blood, which abounds in the streets, must be collected and preserved as a treasure for the future.

Tuesday, 3 November [1942]. When I came home from school, my mother told me several things that she had experienced and heard. My mother sews for a German woman. The German woman is so kind, so refined, that the female workers like her very much. She gave my mother soap, flour, candy and bread. She is interested in life in the ghetto. She sympathises wholeheartedly with the Jews in the ghetto. "The war will end, it's all the Führer's fault. You will be liberated, you are needed, you are useful, hard-working people. We Germans and you Jews will not suffer much longer." A second story:

in the Wierzbolow labour camp a German was beating a Jew with a stick. German soldiers passing by jumped out of their truck and tore the stick away from the hooligan and angrily asked him:

It warms the spirit to think that among the German masses there are those who sympathise with us

"Why are you beating him? You dog, you probably haven't been to the front. So you beat. If you had seen how blood flows like water, you wouldn't beat …" These stories sound half-legendary. Every Jew in the ghetto likes to expand, enrich stories like that. People delight in them. For example, they tell that a German tore the yellow star off a Jew, saying that such patches will soon not be needed! All these stories circulated among the people. Everyone alters them, strengthens the effect, embellishes them. But the spark of truth is in them. It warms the spirit to think that among the German masses there are those who sympathise with us and feel our pain and their shame.

At home, we were told about unrest in Poland. They say that Radom has been captured by Polish rebels. Fifty Poles were hanged in Warsaw. But these are all insubstantial rumours.

Wednesday, 4 [November 1942]. In the evening the news becomes known in the ghetto: the commander of a group of forest workers was shot dead by partisans. The news interested me. Everyone tells something different. Finally you end up with the following: the commander of a group of forest workers, a policeman, behaved badly towards the workers. In the area there were partisans who found out about the behaviour of the commander towards his brothers and decided that whoever beats his brother is an enemy. Yesterday, in the evening, they came to his lodgings and shot him. This morning he was brought to Vilna. He was still alive and told everything. That sums up what you can get from everyone's stories. There are more details. He was turned to the wall and told not to move. He wanted somehow to justify himself and turned around, so they shot him. This event made a strong impression on me. It was strangely difficult for me to decide whether he deserved to die or not, because while some people said that he was a monster, that he used to beat and bully his fellow Jewish workers, others say that on the contrary he was a kind man who was strict because he was forced to be that way. But one thing I did feel – a triumph, a joy, that hidden in the woods there are those who stand up for the poor, humiliated ghetto Jew and by carrying out their revenge, they have his revenge in mind as well ...

Thursday, 5 [November 1942]. A woman neighbour of ours spent last night in the Lidske Street jail because of the light that could be seen through her windowpane. With her in the jail was a woman who had come from Oshmene, where our "brave" police department put things in order. In brief, in a few words, she described what took place in Oshmene. The Vilna Police ordered all Jews to go to the square in front of the synagogue. But children under the age of ten were to be left at home. The policemen quickly divided the crowd into two groups: one, the able-bodied, were driven into the synagogue, the second, weaker and older people, were taken somewhere. Later it was learned that they were handed over to the Lithuanians. In the evening the Jewish police distributed certificates to those left behind and released them. They went to find the children under the age of ten in their homes. My heart starts to beat strongly when I hear such stories. When you hear that, you feel deep in your soul what the Jews of Oshmene have gone through. That is what makes it so terrifying to hear.

In the morning I went to the ruins. A thick, black piece of a wall is barely standing. Poor, older people work for twelve rubles in these ruins. They take a big rope with a loop and throw it around the wet wall. About twenty old, weak people harness themselves to the rope and pull. The wall leans like a drunken man. The wall sways in the air but does not fall. A lot of men pitch in to help. It makes quite a picture: within the little streets, ruins stick out and a snake-like human chain is desperately tugging at a wall with a rope. The mass of people groan but the wall groans too. After the last pull in the harness, the wall shakes, rolls and crashes into another wall. A hurricane of scattered bricks descends and the whole street, with the people in it, is covered with lime dust. The whole street is flooded with debris. Today we went to 4 Shavler Street with our questionnaire forms for ghetto research. We were not well received and sadly I must confess that they were right. We were reproached for being cool-headed. "You mustn't go poking into other people's wounds. Our lives are clear enough." She's right, but I am not at fault, because I believe that everything must be described and noted down because it will all be taken into account.

Friday, 6 [November 1942]. This morning I stood in line for tickets to the bath. In the street, near the wall, stands a peasant, already wearing his big winter fur coat, his hat covering his ears, in big boots. He has probably come to the ghetto to take care of some business. Next to him stands a boy of about fifteen, also in a peasant overcoat and high boots. From under his peasant cap, two black lively eyes look out. Everyone understands right away: a Jewish boy living as a Christian. Soon a whole circle gathers around him. His neighbours turn up. They ask about his family: there is nobody. He works for the peasant and the peasant gives him food and he lives with him. He looks at everyone and everyone looks at him with astonishment. "Well," he says to a Jewish woman in Russian, "bring the goods, we're leaving soon." In the evening I leave the Club. It's dry and cold and my limbs already are feeling the winter. By the light of the tiny ghetto streetlights, I see little snowflakes, the first snow, a portent of a winter that is already crossing our threshold. Let us hope that this first snow will bring us not cold and sadness, but a swift change.

Saturday, 7 [November 1942]. Today is a beautiful day. The sky is blue, the sun is shining. The air is cold and frosty and already feels like winter. Today is a great anniversary, twenty-five years since the Great October Revolution. It looks as if the outdoors had dressed itself up for the holiday. I stand by the window and think: the Soviet land greets the holiday in bloody, hard struggle. We greet it in the ghetto. The terrible howl of an aeroplane above the building interrupts my thoughts. The steel whistle of the propeller cuts into the air, flies through it and fades away somewhere far, far away. We are already used to the diabolical flying around in the air, to the shocking whistle that fills your head with the horror of war. The new country that is now twenty-five years old is drenched with blood. The seventh of November 1942 has come up bloody and frosty. But I am sure that the victory of October will be victorious again.

In the morning, Gabik came to see me. We agreed to do our homework together today. The room is cold. Gabik tells me about himself. His father is in the hospital. A heart ailment. Their situation is very difficult. I have seen all their hardship from the beginning of the ghetto, when they arrived with small bundles. Gabik is emaciated. He works in the library and receives a double ration card. The work interferes with his studies. I know very well that Gabik is seldom free of hunger. Today Gabik seems a bit melancholy and distracted, though despite his difficult situation he is in good spirits and happy. Gabik hopes that when his father leaves the hospital he will obtain a stable position. It turns out that in the morning they sent for his mother to come to the hospital. Gabik is standing in line to receive his rations, but his mother has the ration cards. He looks for her everywhere, but she's not there and he is very worried. Is she still in the hospital? Why? We do a few assignments and Gabik leaves to look for his mother again. Later he comes back, again disturbed and gloomy. He didn't find her anywhere. We continue with our homework. We started to feel cold. Gabik was restless. I felt along with him that there was something bad happening and the mood made us uncomfortable. The chilly outdoors penetrated our spirits. We closed our notebooks. I was very hungry and so was my friend. We had a bite to eat; the hot bowl of soup made us feel warmer. Meanwhile Lute Shrayber, who lives with Gabik, came in and told him to go home. His mother had returned and was asking him to come home. Gabik became disturbed, let go of his notebooks and nervously asked what had happened. Lute and I exchanged glances. "Not good," I understood. Gabik sensed our looks and when Lute wanted to be the last to leave the room in order to tell me something, Gabik had a premonition and tried to get Lute to leave first. Then, as he ran out the door, he turned his face around. There were tears in his eyes ... I felt a pang in my heart. I remained alone in the little room. Nobody was at home. It was quiet, cold and felt terribly strange. Sadness hovered overhead. I felt so dejected and sad. I thought it over: I had already sensed the terrible thing that is on its way. Aeroplanes brutally whirred in the sky. A little later Tkatsh and Reyze Stolitski came in and told me that Gabik's father is on his deathbed, that we should go over to be with Gabik in the hospital. I felt a cold chill come over me ... What a great misfortune, what a tragedy. I went to the hospital, but they would not let me in. I felt terribly sad. A cold wind lashed my face. In the evening I learned of the expected end. Gabik no longer has a father. I felt how much misfortune is contained in that word. How will Gabik live through it? He is so joyful and light-hearted and suddenly before my eyes he has received this painful blow. In the evening we decided to go see him. Gabik was already in bed. We left him alone. For a time, we stayed in the adjoining room and talked about the misfortune. I experienced a lot. I witnessed the whole sudden tragedy. He had been looking for his mother and at the same time they were looking for him so he could say goodbye to his dying father. I feel a lot of pity for Gabik and for his mother. How terrible is the fate of these quiet, solitary people. How honestly and modestly they lived, quiet and refined. How hard it will be for Gabik now. How much he loved his father. I feel Gabik's misfortune deep in my heart.

Sunday, 8 November [1942]. Today there are two funerals in the ghetto. In the morning there is the funeral of the policeman who was shot. Our police have made a whole ceremony out of this funeral. The coffin stood in the sports field. A cantor sang and a rabbi spoke. Representatives of the labour units and leaders of the police. "He fell at his post, a victim of his duty," we are proud of him. The police march by in their leather coats and new hats. On the dead man's coffin is his policeman's cap and his well-earned "stripes". At his side stand firemen with torches. It is imposing and ceremonial – "a hero". The foolish crowd edges and jostles forward to have a look. I feel sadness in my heart. The walls are plastered with obituary notices. The teacher and scholar Dr Moyshe Heller has died. At a time when the police and others like them carry out ceremonies in the miserable streets, a part of the ghetto grieves over the death of Moyshe Heller. His funeral is today at three o'clock. I want to see Gabik. I can imagine how hard it is for him, all alone. I am still under the painful impression of all the things I witnessed yesterday. During the day they began to let people into the hospital where Dr Moyshe Heller lies. I encountered Gabik there as well. As soon as he saw his friends, his eyes welled up with tears, but he soon calmed down.

We went into the room. Two candles are burning at the head of the bed. Gabik stands with us. I can't look him straight in the

It is becoming emptier and emptier around us

eyes. I have no words for him. So we all stand in oppressive silence with heavy hearts. The whole time I had been wondering what Gabik would look like, what will I see the first time we meet after the misfortune. Gabik is holding up very well. His face expresses gloomy sadness and a bit of bewilderment. He is calm and looks very bad – pale, with dark circles under his eyes. He looks as if he has already become accustomed to it all and is quietly enduring it. In the room a crowd of people gathers – students, teachers and colleagues. The students from the *Kailis* factory [fur factory located outside the ghetto] come in with their teachers and flowers in their hands. He taught there as well. Gabik's mother is crying, but like everything in their lives, quietly, without noise, with feeling. But Gabik is strong. He has really shown a lot of manliness and hardly shed a tear. I like that a lot. The room becomes crowded as people push forward around the coffin. Yashunski and Teacher Kaplan speak about the deceased, characterising him as a man of many talents, a bearer of culture and devoted to Yiddish education and culture. Gabik's father, though a cripple, was a man of healthy spirit and strong character. He loved what was fine, genuine and natural and hated hypocrisy in his own people and in all mankind. Gabik would often tell me about his father – his excursions with him, the healthy education he received from his father. It is becoming emptier and emptier around us. Four of our greatest and best teachers have gone away: Pludermakher, Khayimson, Gershteyn, and Dr Heller was the fourth – victims of the ghetto. The coffin is shut. We want to lead Gabik out, but he wants to stay. Calmly he looks on as they carry out the coffin, but I see in his sadness that the misfortune is deep, deep in his heart. We go back from the gate. It is getting a bit dark. It is cold. There is almost no studying in school. No one is in the mood for it.

Monday, 9 [November 1942]. A winter day. I put on my winter coat, pulled on my boots. I walked through the little ghetto streets.

Snow is falling. The air is frosty. I sensed winter. My cheeks are burning. I walk around and start to feel warmer, and my spirit is good. It seems to me that the first snows foretell something good and encouraging.

In the Yiddish class, our teacher Mire told us about Dr Heller. Teacher Mire went through a lot with Dr Heller's death. The whole time she was with Gabik at his father's side. In the middle of Teacher Mire's talk, Gabik walked into the class. The teacher was not flustered and continued to speak, explaining to Gabik what was going on. Gabik listened along with the rest of us, sad and calm as he has been up to now. Gabik is working again in the library, having obtained his father's position. Gabik is recovering. In the Jewish history class, we have begun preparing the trial of Herod. An interesting piece of work awaits us. I have been chosen as prosecutor and Gabik as Herod.

Tuesday, 10 [November 1942]. Today is a cold day. In the morning I cooked food for myself on our electric burner and did my homework at the same time. The first half of the day passes slowly and I am glad when I go to school. The lectures are quite interesting. In history we learn very interesting things about Rome, in Jewish history about Herod. After school I go to the Club. In the street it is cold, at home it is cold, so you feel like running to the Club where you don't feel anything. Our ghetto-research circle is working actively. We hope that as a result of our efforts we will have a valuable historical piece of work about the courtyard at 4 Shavler Street. Today the founding meeting of the circle for Jewish history took place. We have decided to read and study Jewish history and to deal with the problems of Jewish history that are interesting for us and can be brought up to date, especially Jewish history in recent times. Now we begin with the case of Flavius Josephus. We will prepare a trial of him as well. I have also been chosen as a leader of the literary circle. We are collecting folklore materials. With so much work to do, you don't feel the cold. I go home from the Club. People are running, huddled against the cold. It is dark and sinister. On the corners, under the sad, dark ghetto streetlights, it is more lively. Under this light, like flies around a lantern, huddle the poor ghetto vendors, mostly children. The bluish, dull light shines on the rags of the children and women, shines on the red little hands, frozen by the cold, that are counting the money and giving change. Frozen, with their shelves on their backs, they edge towards the little bit of the corner that is illuminated. They stand like that until the curfew sounds, then they disappear with their little shelves of merchandise into the dark ghetto streets. In the morning you see them again in the gloomy light, stamping their feet and breathing into their frozen hands. I run down the cold, sad ghetto street and run home and straight into bed, to fall asleep faster, because when you sleep, you dream and your hopes are sweeter than when you are awake.

Wednesday, 11 [November 1942]. In school and at the Club we have a lot of work. We have finished our Yiddish textbook. We have to prepare three reports. 1. Scenes of poverty in Avrom Reyzen 2. Jewish children in Avrom Reyzen 3. Jewish children at work. In addition, in Jewish history, we are preparing the trial of Herod. The trial will be public. We have a court, a prosecutor, a defender, the accused and a whole series of personages from history as witnesses. We have already distributed the share of the work among ourselves. Now I have the hardest work ahead of me – to write up the indictment and prepare a series of questions for the witnesses for the prosecution. We need to study Graetz, Dubnow and others. There is lively and interesting work going on in school now.

Thursday, 12 [November 1942]. It is cold. Winter is coming on strong and brutal. It is cold at home. In the morning it is still dark when we get up. You don't feel like getting out of bed. The windowpanes are decorated with frost. Winter is the cruellest time of year for the ghetto inhabitants. The homes are without stoves, without windows, we have no firewood and clothing. We do not heat our stove. It doesn't pay to heat it as it gives hardly any warmth. We should try to install a small iron stove. One of our windowpanes is broken. We also have very little wood. It is too cold for me to stand in the kitchen and cook. I take the meals to be cooked in the bakery. I put in potatoes, peas and pearl barley and a small piece of meat and it's excellent. In the ghetto they are distributing potatoes, 10 kilograms for each person. I stood in line for half a day today and did not get any. During that time I got good and frozen. Dozens of people stand in line. I look at my fellow standers-in-line. They stand in the cold in worn old clothes. Around you, you only see faces that are bluish from the cold. Nearby there is a commotion. Women are quarrelling, cursing each other, stamping on their feet. During the first hour, they gave out pretty good potatoes. Later they began to hand out potatoes that were frozen and wet. Freezing, I went back home. I decided it wasn't worthwhile accepting them. We have enough potatoes, brought from the labour unit. I wasted half a day and got frozen. At home it's cold too. I am barely able to warm myself with a bowl of soup. The cold casts a shadow of sadness over my heart. I am home alone. I don't feel like doing anything. I hold on until it is time to go to class. It's cold there too, but when you are studying it feels warmer somehow. What gloom descends on the ghetto with the arrival of winter. People run trembling and groaning through the streets. Everyone has his worries. In the evening, things turn happy. The workers came with happy, good, reliable news.

An American landing force has disembarked in West Africa. Tunis, Algiers and Morocco. Spain and Portugal have received ultimatums not to interfere with the operation. The Anglo–American forces have begun a major operation against the

German and Italian army in Africa. They are moving against the Germans from two sides. In the east the English are attacking from Egypt and in the west the Americans are moving from Tunis into Tripolitania. The Germans are receiving terrible blows. The German–Italian army faces the danger of falling into the sea. The Americans are operating with a strong air force and navy. After a big battle the Americans and the English captured Tobruk, Sallum and a series of other positions. The Vichy Government ordered the French navy and land army to put up resistance against the English and Americans. On the part of the French, no resistance arose. The Anglo–American fleet operates freely in the Mediterranean and a landing has taken place also in Corsica. The Germans fear an invasion in France and have taken over Unoccupied France. Landings in Italy are expected.

It is true that what is happening in Africa is far from us. But people say that the operation of liquidating the Germans in Africa is in accordance with the demands of the Soviet Union, because when the English are finished in Africa, we can expect a second front in Europe. And then … we may be able to leave the ghetto. You feel warmer hearing that the battle goes on, that the spark of our hope still glows.

Saturday, 14 [November 1942]. Today I stayed home all day. I got good and frozen and, as it happens, not in line for potatoes but writing my Yiddish essay. Gabik Heller and I composed our first Yiddish essay. It's no great pleasure to sit in one place in the cold and think.

Sunday, 15 November [1942]. Today our home is in a state of upheaval. Our neighbours are installing an iron stove. They demand that we open the second door to our room, so they can block the door that we use now with a cabinet. Otherwise, they say, they won't be able to mark out a space for the oven. We have to give in to them. The room is chaos. We are moving our sideboard. Clothes are scattered all over. Today, locksmiths are working in the house to change the locks (we will now have a separate entrance through the kitchen). A carpenter is fixing the window frames and glaziers are repairing the windowpanes. Each of them is banging and yelling. It's hell.

Monday, 16 [November 1942]. Classes in school are not running normally now. In the next few days we will be transferring our studies to 21 Daytshe Street, our new premises.

Tuesday, 17 [November 1942]. All day today I sat reading Dubnow's history, "picking" material for the trials of Herod and Flavius Josephus. The work is very interesting.

Wednesday, 18 [November 1942]. Today we already held our classes at 21 Daytshe Street. We study from 8.45 to 12. The classrooms are big and attractive and remind us of our old school. But today it was still very cold.

Friday, 20 [November 1942]. Today at my parents' workplace things were very jolly. A German in tatters came in, almost naked. Partisans had stripped him of his clothes. He came with a note saying to put clothes on him. The Jewish workers laughed their heads off. My mother often tells me about her relationships with German women. And they tell her about their lives as well. "My blouse needs to be black," [a German woman] said, because yesterday her husband was killed and tomorrow a brother will fall and then a father and so on and so forth. The German people must be in mourning.

Monday, 23 [November 1942]. Today at our house they built a range. By chance, the electricity was cut off. They work on the range by candlelight. The room is full of clay and bricks. And in the middle of the commotion there's me with my scribbling. Lately I have a mass of work from school and the Club. I spend whole days with history books. We are preparing various reports and trials. In addition, I am in charge of the circle for creative original writing with the poet Sutskever and I have to be in constant contact with him. The study period in the morning is quite agreeable, but the rest of the day rushes past quickly. I don't even have time to finish my book from the library. I have presentation after presentation in Yiddish and history to worry about. And it's all happening at the same time. Every evening, as usual, I go to the Club, visit the history circles, the nature circle and the literary ones. I often stay for the try-outs of the dramatic circle – it's happy, cheerful. We wait impatiently for the completion of our space on Disner Street.

Tuesday, 24 [November 1942]. The mood in the ghetto is upbeat and among us young people it's the same. The ghetto reverberates with good news, the ghetto radiates with hope: people think it's starting to look like any minute we'll be leaving our prison ... The Americans are advancing towards Tunis. The French fleet in Dakar has surrendered. From the south the South African army is attacking the Germans. Rome is being bombed constantly. Most importantly, the German army has suffered a defeat at Stalingrad. Two Soviet armies have converged, encircling the enemy in the Stalingrad–Rostov region. Thousands of Germans killed and taken prisoner. The Soviets are also attacking strongly on the Central Front. The ghetto feels, with all its senses, that the end is approaching, or rather that our beginning is coming.

In the evening I strolled around the ghetto streets. It's a wintry evening, with a hint of frost and a clear sky. The snow sparkles here and there where it hasn't been trampled on. The evening is refreshing ... It makes me feel so light-hearted. The evening has sort of enchanted me. The ruins on Yatkever Street shimmer as if covered in diamonds. It is quiet and empty. The snow-covered ruins stand under a blue frosty sky where a big, round moon hovers and reveals itself from time to time through a different hole in the ruin walls. On such evenings I used to love to stroll, two friends together, in a quiet spot outside the city. It is so pleasant when your cheeks are burning, when you breathe in the frosty evening freshness. I feel the same way today, though along

On such a night I can imagine that soon something new will happen

the way I encounter a ruin. But in my heart I am in a strangely good mood, because on such a night I can imagine that soon something new will happen ... I feel it is nearby, I can touch it in the frost with my hand.

Wednesday, 25 [November 1942]. Today in the ghetto the day began with commotion, panic and terror. The gates are locked, the streets blocked, the ghetto cooperative closed, all the employees of the Jewish Council detained in the theatre, with their certificates confiscated. The ghetto is deathly quiet. Hundreds of people lay in *malines* today. It felt like a storm was about to descend on the ghetto. It all ended with a big laugh. Gens notified Mushkat that he should check, with the help of the employees of the Jewish Council, who in the ghetto population is not going to work. Wanting to assemble the Jewish Council employees, Mushkat took away their certificates. His "organisational talents" created a terrible panic and the laughter is because he himself ended up in Lidske Street jail.

Thursday, 26 [November 1942]. Today I deposited a pot in the bakery. In the evening I came to retrieve it. It's not possible, because Murer is at the gate. I was barely able to make my way to the bakery. It turns out that our dignitaries also put things in the warming oven. As soon as they started pulling the hot black pots out of the oven a big commotion broke out over Major Frukht's baked pudding and Commander Mushkat's pot – they must be put back in the oven *sofort* [immediately], so they won't, God forbid, get cold. Meanwhile we hear the news that things are very bad at the gate. Beatings and confiscations. The ghetto is already used to that. Nevertheless, the ghetto starts to tremble right away. "They are beating at the gate" – these words fall gaspingly and desperately from the mouths of the workers who are coming, dishevelled and upset, from whom can be heard a kind of humming shriek. Blackened people stream past, wild screams, a whip pounds … They are beating at the gate. Jewish policemen, on Murer's orders, are beating and confiscating the little piece of bread that the Jewish worker is carrying.

Friday, 27 [November 1942]. Today I spent the whole afternoon carrying clay for the Club. They are finally installing a stove there.

Monday, 30 [November 1942]. The ghetto is buzzing with good news. The Soviets have broken through the front in Latvia near Velikie Luki. They're coming, they're coming, closer and closer.

Tuesday, 1 December [1942]. Today in school we had an assignment in class on the topic of "Images of Poverty". I wrote extensively. I brought Reyzen's stories up to date, related them to us and ended by saying that the ghetto is the final stage of generations of poverty. We will be the ones who will come out of the ghetto and throw off the poverty that for generations has oppressed the Jewish people.

Friday, 4 December [1942]. My mother is not well and for that reason I couldn't go to school. Naturally I spent the day among the pots and pans. It's a lot easier for me now. I cook on the iron burners. When you heat them, it gets warm in the room. Because

I'm studying, the cooking and housekeeping have started to get on my nerves. I'm getting a little lazy doing them. Today I cooked lentils with meatballs for lunch and brought my mother gargling water and tea. In the afternoon I picked up the school assignments and went to the Club. In the Club, among my friends in the various sections, you feel refreshed after such a tedious day.

Saturday, 5 [December 1942]. The white of winter has slipped in even to us in the ghetto. It snows and snows and envelops the dark ghetto alleys in whiteness. Children are delighted with the whiteness, though you don't see that much of it in the ghetto. Still, it is enough. The ruin at the corner of Yatkever and Disner streets is covered in snow, creating hills and valleys and youngsters go sledding on them. In the evening I have a lot of work. I am rewriting my indictment of Herod. There are a lot of assignments. In school we have added the subjects of chemistry and geography. I desperately don't want to stay at home. I feel like going for a walk. I walk over to the sports field. I stand there all alone under the big starry sky. By moonlight you can see how diamonds fall from the sky. The sports field is covered in white snow. I breathe in deeply and feel the frosty freshness. I set off running over the crunchy snow. How I love the crunch of the snow. I remember, in the good old days, an excursion with sleds. At Belmont [hill], our teacher Biber climbs up the mountain with us. Our cheeks are burning and the snow is constantly crunchy under our feet. Under the hills, the wintry landscape stretches in frosty splendour. I stand at the peak of the hill and breathe so freely. Now, standing in the sports field in the ghetto, I breathe in like that as well. Now in the ghetto I sense the magic of winter. I go home – it's already late, soon it will be the curfew whistle. On the street corners a few vendors are still standing with boxes hanging on them. There are three of us in the street. I head for home and a passer-by buys something from a poor little girl. By the light of the street lantern, she gives him change with her frozen, blue little fingers. By the light of the lantern I see how her hand trembles, how her whole little body shakes. She is totally unable to count the money. I run home fast because I hear the curfew whistle.

Sunday, 7 [actually 6 December 1942]. At our ghetto-research circle we have decided once and for all to finish the hard work, that is, to go around to the homes with the questionnaires. We want to start going over the answers and, on the basis of the materials, to create history. Today my friend and I were in a new home. They gave us good answers. Going like that among the people of the ghetto and talking to them about their life we get to see the ghetto individual, how he thinks and speaks, his psychology. Generally, we don't require the family name. But there are people who want the family name written down. They want it to go down in history. Others, on the contrary, are terribly careful and exceptionally diplomatic and not a word is beside the point. Every word is weighed and measured. If you ask them where they lived before the ghetto, they do not answer; if you ask in which labour unit they work, they do not answer. They look at us as if we were tax collectors. The ghetto resident is full of distrust.

Conversely, today, for example, simple Jews answered us in such a friendly and agreeable way. They were interested in answering us. [They may not have understood it, but] still they felt with all their heart that they ought to answer us. They poured out their hearts for us, spelled out with all the details of all their misfortunes, the complicated tragedies of adding names to their certificates. "What do you say, children, this is what that Führer has made of us, may they make the same of him. That will be our history. Write, write, children, it's good that you're doing that." We finish interviewing a family and say thank you. "Oh, don't thank us, promise us that we will leave the ghetto and we will tell you three times as much, poor wretches that we are." We assured the woman ten times that we will leave the ghetto.

In the evening we had a new complication. My mother bought a bath ticket for her labour unit. The men's tickets were given to the women and the reverse happened with the women's tickets. There was a danger that the tickets would become worthless. But as it happened the men and women went at the same time (to two baths) and they switched with one another. Meanwhile there was much laughter during the entry into the baths. People were running back and forth. The baths are the place for news and politics. Of course first place goes to the teahouse, but today there was news in the bath. People told about various Jewish misfortunes. The ghetto in Postov was set on fire. People tell of pogroms, of Jews who wander around in the forests and are shot as partisans. They need to be rescued and other such sad things.

Monday, 8 [actually 7 December 1942]. Late in the evening we go home from the Club. It is long after the curfew whistle. The street is deserted. The snow crunches under your feet. The little ghetto streets are enveloped in night and frost. I come to a street crossing. From a dark corner a policeman appears. He approaches, his wooden soles banging in the silence. "Pass," he grumbles. I give him the password and he pauses under the light of a street lamp. Suddenly a dog runs out of the darkness. We both look at it as if it were some kind of strange wonder. The policeman calls it and whistles to it, but seeing him it lowers its frozen tail and runs back into the darkness. The policeman laughs: "Didn't have a pass!"

Wednesday, 9/Thursday, 10 December [1942]. I realise that today is my birthday. Today I turned fifteen. We don't even realise how time flies, how it runs ahead unnoticed and disappears. Then you realise all of a sudden, as I did today, for example, that days and months go by, that the ghetto is not a painful blink of an eye in a dream that will dissipate at any moment, but is a great swamp in which you lose your days and weeks. Today I was deeply lost in thought. I have decided that in the ghetto I will not waste my time doing nothing and I feel fortunate in a way that I study, read and develop and see to it that time does not stand still as I go along with it in a normal way. In the day-to-day life in the ghetto it seems to me that I am living normally, but I often get a kind of pang in my heart. After all, I could have lived better. Do I really have to see that bricked-in ghetto gate, and in the best days of my life must I really just see one alley, a few stuffy courtyards? More and different thoughts get tangled up, but I feel two things most strongly: a regret, a kind of nagging feeling. I wish to cry out to time to wait, not to run. I wish to take back the year that has passed and keep it for later, for my new life. The second thing that I feel today is strength and *hope*. I do not feel despair in the least. Today I turned fifteen and live very much for tomorrow. I do not feel two ways about it. I see before me sun and sun and sun …

Thursday, 10/Friday, 11 December [1942]. Today there was a Club holiday in the kitchen at 6 Rudnitsker Street. We felt like having a good time, so we managed to get hold of 100 kilograms of potatoes and we baked a pudding. Today was the happiest evening that I have spent in the ghetto.

At nine o'clock we gathered in the kitchen. Now we're all seated at the tables. Many guests have come and now we sit tightly packed together. I look around at those present. All of them our nearest and dearest teachers, friends and comrades. It feels so intimate, so warm, so pleasant. This evening we showed who we are and what we can do. The bunch from the Club presented songs and declamations. Till late at night we sang along with the adults songs that tell of youthfulness and hope. Very fine was the "living newspaper" in which the Club, its chairman and its experts were humorously criticised. We sat at the bare tables and dined on potato pudding and coffee. We were so happy, so happy. Song after song echoed. It is already twelve o'clock. We are as if intoxicated by the joy of youth. No one wants to go home. Songs are bawled out that simply do not want to stop. Late at night we disperse. Today we have proved that we are young. "Behind walls, but nevertheless young, young forever" is our slogan with which we "march towards the sun". Today we have shown that even in the three little streets we can maintain our youthful fervour. We have shown that it will not be a broken youth that will emerge from the ghetto. From the ghetto will emerge a strong, hardened and spirited youth.

Sunday, 13 [December 1942]. In the streets there's a thaw. A wet snow is falling and the streets are wet and muddy. In the mud, a long line of people are standing at the "Rute" food cooperatives. Today they are giving out potatoes and horsemeat. Two wagons are standing at the store, one with wet, frozen potatoes, the other with red, bloody horsemeat. The potatoes are dumped into the cellars. Flocks of women and ragged children chase after the potatoes that have fallen into the mud. A policeman chases them away. But right away they throw themselves again on the few falling potatoes. The policeman curses. "They won't even let you take frozen potatoes," complains a woman with a yellow, hungry face. Around the wagon with the horsemeat there's something going on as well. Ragged little fellows with burning eyes are hanging around the wagon. They are saying something to the driver of the wagon, a Christian boy in a padded coat and big, heavy boots and with a big whip. I soon see what is going on. The Christian boy rummages around in the meat, tears a piece off the end and puts it in the pocket of the Jewish boy.

Wednesday, 16 [December 1942]. In the evening when they come home from work and have eaten, people start to talk about life at work outside the ghetto. The various images and conversations with Germans and plain old stories are very interesting. In the *Schneiderstube* a German, when he is hungry, will say, "I want to stuff myself like a Jew." For them, the Jew is the embodiment of hunger. They think the Jews feel only hunger. My mother dealt with a German woman who came with a little girl. The little girl asked to go pee-pee. When my mother told her that the bathroom was pretty far away in the courtyard, the German woman told the little girl to do it right on the spot. She explained to the little child that often the Jews in the ghetto also have nowhere outside to go, so they do it on the spot. It may seem like a silly case, but it shows what it has come to when German women use us as an example for their children of people who are unfortunate and suffering. In a labour unit, a German argues constantly that the Jews are responsible for the war. Behind his back, the Jewish workers make fun of him. Among the workers there is an older man and the others pick on him: "Tsalke, you hear, the *yeke* [German] says you are responsible for the war." The old Jew interrupts his work for a moment and grumbles: "May evil fall on his head. So I'm the one who's responsible for the war!"

Saturday, 19 [December 1942]. Today there's new turmoil in the ghetto. The ghetto is agitated and worried. Twenty men who work in Soltanishok were detained at the gate because flour was found on them. On the orders of Murer they were immediately taken away to Lukishki Prison.

Lukishki Prison is the most terrifying word in the ghetto. People seldom come back from there, and twenty Jews have already been torn away from us. This afternoon they were suddenly brought to the ghetto and put into the Lidske Steet jail. But right away Murer arrived and gave the order that they be immediately taken to Lukishki. That is how they teased the ghetto and at the end tore away twenty Jews.

Sunday, 20 [December 1942]. Today the ghetto schools went to have a look at part of the "Plastic Plan" [three-dimensional model] of the city of Vilna, which is being created in the ghetto as a gift to the *Gebietskommissar*. The Plan will cover 20 square metres. The hardest work has already been done. What's been accomplished may be only a small part of the city, but it is the most important part and the hardest to carry out. Under a projector, the centre of Vilna lies before us on a table. On plaster of Paris plates, on a scale of 1:2500, every little house, every little street is outlined. Everything is beautifully tinted and shows exceptional workmanship. The children rush to look at the model and naturally they all look for their own house, the street from which they came to the ghetto. Engineer Durmashkin points things out for us: that's the Viliye [River], the Green Bridge, Shnipishok and here is the cathedral. The children gaze, as if hungry, at the lovely hilly lanes around the Viliye and Vilenke, from which they were expelled. The Plastic Plan of Vilna is truly a great work of art, of which we can be proud, because it couldn't have been created outside the ghetto. Only a Jew, in the present moment, can provide the effort and patience that went into this work. Seeing our work, we can be sure that we will yet see the beautiful streets of Vilna not just in a model, but also in reality.

Monday, 22 [actually 21 December 1942]. Finally, today at eight in the evening, the trial of Herod is taking place. In our temporary clubhouse a big audience has assembled – guests, Club members. I gave the opening statement for the prosecution. The trial was weak in certain respects. The discussions between the two parties were weak and you could tell that some of the responses had been coached. But in general, our trial proved successful. It was quite imposing: our chairman, the court, the cross-examination of the historical figures who appeared as witnesses. The speeches included a great deal of rich material and were beautifully carried out. I accused Herod of a two-faced policy, of playing the role of a Roman agent, for introducing into the country Roman customs that were hostile and alien to the Jewish spirit. I accused him of killing the people. The defence pointed to Herod's positive actions, declared that Herod lived in a stormy time, his behaviour was against his will, that many of his deeds were for the good of the Jewish people. The court chose a committee of experts, teachers and historians, that would answer the question of whether Herod's actions were in the interests of the people. There began a great discussion among the adults, which was the most interesting of all. Various opinions were expressed. The defence position was strong. School Director Turbovitsh took a stand in favour of the defence of Herod. In his opinion Herod's actions were in the interests of the people, because the revolt against Rome would have hastened the disaster. Many of the experts took a middle-of-the-road stand. Teachers Karbatshnik and Gordon sided with the prosecution. The closing of the trial and the discussion in the hall were very interesting and dragged on till late at night. The verdict was delivered: Herod was declared guilty. The verdict confirms my opinion. In general, the trial made a good impression. Students in the ghetto are engaged in a more profound historical issue, how to analyse a personage as complicated as Herod.

Wednesday, 23 [December 1942]. In the evening I went to the literary circle. Leo Bernshteyn lectured on the topic of German literature. It was very interesting. Leaving the circle, I felt that he gave me a lot. I became acquainted with a part of literary history.

Thursday, 24 [December 1942]. On a walk this evening I ran into my friend Mulke Lurie. He was coming back from work, wearing big boots and carrying a sack. Mulke has suffered a lot in the ghetto. With no parents, he had been staying up to now with an uncle. Now the uncle is not supporting him. I try to find out why, but he won't tell me. I questioned him about his life, who is supporting him. He has a little money from before because he did a little trading. Now he works in the *Soldatenheim* [Soldiers' Home], an excellent labour unit. "Where do you eat?" I ask him. He explains that at work there is no shortage of food. Three times a day you are fed from the kitchen and in addition you get something from the Germans' own pot. It's got a bit more fat in it than the Jewish one. "And if they don't give you anything, you take it on your own," Mulke concludes with a bitter chuckle. "But what do you eat at home?" I ask him. He tells me that at work he has a box for bread that the Germans give him and honey as well. So he takes the bread and honey with him and he has something for breakfast before he leaves for work. "And now what will you eat?" I ask him. "Now I'm going to eat with some acquaintances, as I've done up to now. Excellent meals and afterward I drink a glass of tea there." I ask him: "Do you have the money to pay for the meal?" "I don't eat for free!" he exclaims, half-offended. Mulke brings potatoes for them that he gets, apparently for free, at work. Mulke seems sad somehow. Six kilograms of potatoes were confiscated from him at the gate. Nevertheless, he was able to bring in 3 kilograms. But he is upset and asks my advice. Should he take the potatoes to the acquaintances for the meal, or should he sell them, because he needs the money very much. "I need to buy a pair of wooden-soled shoes. My boots are soaked. It's a pity, I won't have anything to walk in." I tell him to do what he thinks best. "Well, so be it," Mulke says after hesitating for a few seconds. "I'll sell tomorrow's potatoes and give them over this time." We say goodbye and Mulke disappears into a dark little court on Shpitalne Street where he eats his meals. Soon he will cross the street to where his uncle lives and fall into bed. Tomorrow off to work and then the same thing over again. It made me feel very sad.

Saturday, 26 [December 1942]. Finally, the remodelling of our clubhouse on 4 Disner Street has been completed. We clean the clubhouse and are delighted with it. All the Club members are coming to the opening of our second home.

Sunday, 27 [December 1942]. Today a Mendele commemoration took place in the ghetto. In school we have been reading Mendele. The ghetto is celebrating the twenty-fifth anniversary of the death of Mendele. The commemoration began at twelve o'clock. The speakers dwelled on Mendele as the grandfather of Yiddish literature. Mendele loved the common people. He chastised and criticised them, but only like a father. Mendele believed in the people. He had hopes for the masses, for the simple folk who were so dear to his heart. Mendele's role as a critic of Jewish society was emphasised. During the speech by Teacher Lubotski, a sudden, terribly deplorable incident took place which upset the audience and left an unpleasant aftertaste. In the middle of Teacher Lubotski's talk, the curtain was closed. Teacher Lubotski, backstage, was furious. The curtain opened and the chairman, Yashunski, apologised and stated that this was an accident, a mistake on the part of a stagehand. The audience was in an uproar. It was understood that this was not accidental. From his seat, Kaplan-Kaplanski cried out that the chairman was responsible for everything. Accusations were hurled. They have dared to insult the representative of the Yiddish educators and the real Vilna Jewish intelligentsia. They say that it was the odious behaviour of the performers who were impatient for the talks to end. In order to speed up the time for their performance they resorted to this incident, spoiling for a time the Mendele celebration, which today is uniting all Jewish communities. The artistic program was fine, but lacking in solemnity. The commemoration took place on the ghetto level. The actor Segal, by his actions, showed himself to be on the level of a degraded ghetto Jew.

Monday, 28 [December 1942]. Today it is a sad evening in the ghetto. The streets are full of misfortunes and hard trials: Murer is active at the gate. The street is cordoned off. The exhausted workers returning from work are intercepted at the gate and detained. Today Murer ordered that Jewish workers be strip-searched. The workers were driven into a room and, half-naked and under whips, led to inspection. Their money was confiscated. My uncle walks in. He is coming from the gate, saddened. Eight hundred rubles were taken from him, probably the last money he has. Exhausted and embittered, he tells us of the horror and pain that is taking place now. He had hidden the rubles in his boots and when he had to take off his boots, he threw the money into a corner. Who did this have to happen to? To my uncle, who lives in such poverty. My uncle's misfortunes lie heavily on my heart, along with all the last-minute news from the hell at the gate. A sad evening, a ghetto evening ...

Friday, 1 January 1943. The first day of the year 1943. In honour of the new year the world dressed up white overnight. A white, clear winter day. Today the new year begins. The ghetto encountered the new year with one wish: to be freed from the hated ghetto. The ghetto looks to the new year for salvation, for the dreamed-of liberation. Elke, the young son of Khane-Rone, lives at 4 Shavler Street. (They used to live together with us.) Every day he slips out from [the ghetto] and brings in potatoes and flour through a *maline*. The family is large, so the little boy tries to find ways to survive. A few days ago he was caught by the Jewish police and they gave the small, thin Elke twenty-five lashes. Four policemen held him and Levas himself, the commandant of the gate guards, pitilessly and murderously beat him. The bad little breadwinner was brought home badly flogged.

And Levas is getting married today. The ghetto is an uproar – Levas is getting married. That dog was lately somewhat in danger. Murer had taken a dislike to him. But he demonstrated such cruelty towards his own brothers, stripping them naked at the gate, humiliating and insulting them, taking away their last penny, all for the sake of satisfying Murer. And the Jews are told that by his atrocities he saved the ghetto. Levas was a hit with Murer and

The Jews are told that by his atrocities he saved the ghetto

now he is happy and celebrating his wedding with great pomp. The ghetto hates Levas. It may be that Levas was forced to beat, but the people have to hate the person who is beating and humiliating every day at the gate. The depressed, embittered ghetto Jew is unable to figure out that maybe Levas was beating against his will; the Jew at the gate feels the blow of Levas's whip and he feels hatred towards Levas as a traitor. And today is the day of Levas's lavish wedding, so the people curse him. They say with bitter humour that Levas unwillingly beat his father-in-law at the gate.

Saturday, 2 [January 1943]. In the newspaper today there is a greeting from the *Reichskommissar* to the population. The proclamation says that the German people do not know what the future will bring, but one thing is clear to him – victory belongs to the German people. Therefore the slogan for 1943 is: *Mit dem Führer zum Sieg!* My father tells me that as a reply to that, the walls on the street where he works the slogan appears in big letters: "*Deutschland wohin gehstu?*" [in incorrect German: "Germany, where are you going?"] and after that, "*9 November-1918-Wiwat!*" [The date refers to the abdication of the Kaiser at the end of World War I: "Hurrah"].

Sunday, 3 [January 1943]. Today we received our oral evaluations for the first third of the school year. I got Fives in Yiddish, Jewish history, history and biology. In mathematics, Hebrew, drawing and physics I got Fours. In German and Latin, Threes.

The evaluations ought perhaps to have been better, but even the abovementioned ones show that my time is being wasted on trifles.

Tuesday, 5 [January 1943]. Things are uneasy. In the *Schneiderstube* labour unit they are now laying people off. My father is threatened with a layoff as well. The workers come back upset from work where things are in an uproar. People run, they beg not to be *entlassen* [dismissed]. People try to use *protektsye* ["pull"]. And this commotion is carried over into our home. You hear non-stop nothing but layoffs and certificates and over again the same thing. People seem somehow to have lost the habit of thinking of anything else. Each person carries on his own struggle for existence. People have become so cheap. They have become enslaved to their *Einheiten* [labour units] and if they are dismissed that is the heaviest blow.

Wednesday, 6 [January 1943]. A snowy, cloudy day. The whole ghetto is draped in white. It is dusk, the snow is falling thickly. People come from work. From the gate they disperse through the little streets. The snow-covered hats, collars and sacks gleam white against the dark walls. Suddenly a noise, a commotion. People are not allowed on Rudnitsker Street. Two snow-covered workers call out as they arrive: "Murer is at the gate!"

Thursday, 7 [January 1943]. Today they are giving out 5 deka-grams of pork on the ration cards. I stood in line for a short time and finally I am in the shop. In the ghetto we see among us Jews so much injustice, so much incorrectness, so much that is disgusting – during the distribution of meat on the ration cards, for example. People freeze while standing in line. Policemen and big shots walk in freely. While handing out, the butcher throws a piece of meat to a person who stands in line as if he is doing him a favour. He takes advantage of a child or a shy person, gives them the worst. Conversely, whoever has *protektsye* with the butcher (in the ghetto people sink to the lowest level for the sake of *protektsye*, because in the ghetto Vitamin P, as it is called – P for *protektsye* or *pleytses* [shoulders], meaning *strong* shoulders – always wins), he gets a rather fattier piece. In the shop they're handing out the few dekagrams of pork. Every now and then a policeman walks in, or an "official", a genteel lady or madam, people with briefcases. They turn to the supervisor of the shop or directly to the butcher to "take care of it". It's sickening how the butcher turns his sweetly flattering face to them and cuts out for them a piece of white, fat lard (which I think they have enough of at home). The crowd of frozen women standing in line, silent, furious, devour the table of meat with their eyes. They watch mutely as one person gets the fatty meat and another the bones. People are used to that already. "It's probably too good for you!" yells the butcher at a poor young woman who would also like a better piece of meat. A policeman with a virtuous look on his face wraps a piece of fatty meat in paper.

Today is the opening of the clubhouse. Finally, our club-house is ready. We have finally created a home for ourselves in the ghetto. A warm hall, a workroom that also serves as a read-ing room and a door for the secretary's office. That is our space.

It is ours and in it we will survive the ghetto. Today is the public opening, but unfortunately the Club members will not be present. The dramatic circle will perform for a special invited audience.

Friday, 8 [January 1943]. They are now accepting new students in the technical school in the ghetto. I am struggling within myself: should I go learn a trade or continue to study in the high school as I have up to now. I can't decide. On the one hand, it's wartime. At this moment it's easier for someone who has some skill or other in hand. I'm growing up and sooner or later I will have to go to work. On the other hand, I imagine that going to the technical school will mean interrupting my studies, because after the four-month course the goal is to go to work and if I go to work, I will never return to study in school again. After long hesitation and reflection, I have decided to take advantage of every moment. I have to study, I still have suitable conditions, so I must not call it quits. The desire to study has become a kind of defiance of today, a time that detests studying and loves toil and drudgery. No, I decided, I live with tomorrow not with today and if out of a hundred ghetto youth of my age, ten are able to study, I have to be among the lucky ones. I have to take advantage of that. Studying has become even more precious to me than before.

Today is the first public performance of the Club. We are putting on the beautifully staged number "The Enchanted Little Tailor", "Guards" by Peretz, "Dolls", performed by the Children's Club and "Revolt", a Hebrew recitation. Our dramatic circle has well earned its "Bravo!" Under the difficult conditions of the Club, they staged several really beautiful numbers, which as a group are at the level of a peacetime performance, with make-up, recitations and lighting.

Saturday, 9 [January 1943]. Today is the big Club festival. Our fresh new space is filled with our members and guests. Our hall proudly shows its own stage, with a transparent curtain and reflectors. Several beautiful pictures hang on the wall. In the hall it is warm and pleasant. Between the recently painted walls there hovers a feeling of culture and goodness. "Between Walls, Yet Young", reads the headline of our wall newspaper, which shines down from the wall. A splendid newspaper. The articles are in the shape of walls and a street leading to the ghetto gate. The entire look of the newspaper symbolises the headline and the content of the articles and poems likewise prove that the headline is correct. An excellent bulletin summarises the work that has been accomplished.

Finally, people take their seats. On our own stage sits a board of our own people, our young manager and comrade Leo Bernshteyn, thanks to whose work we achieved the Club, our heroic president

Avreml, Reyze our secretary and a whole assembly of lecturers. The mood is uplifted. Greetings and speeches. Gifts are presented to Leo Bernshteyn and Reyze. Teacher Rokhl Broydo spoke well: "When a people has a youth, it is a sign of the progress of the people. We have a youth whose banner is bloodied and red, but we hold it fast. The youth in the ghetto is the firm bridge to the future!"

We applaud long and hard.

Until twelve at night our dramatic circle showed what it was capable of. It's a pleasure to see my friends perform. We have every right to be proud of them. Such beautiful numbers, decorations and costumes. And everything so well and consistently carried out. A gift is presented to Pilnik, the favourite of the Club, the chimney sweep–director who staged the performance. Till half past two we stayed in the Club, intoxicated by the joy of youth. After the program we had some entertainment, a living newspaper, songs, recitations. Pilnik delivers one song after another. We are young, our young hall is filled to the brim with the joy and work of youth. Our spirit, which we proudly hold high within the walls of the ghetto, will be the finest gift to the future which now arises. Long live Youth: the progress of our people.

Sunday, 10 [January 1943]. At last we have an iron stove in the classroom. We've been freezing long enough! We heat it with abandon and it's warm, a pleasure.

Wednesday, 13 [January 1943]. I go into a house. A Jew from Braslav, a town in White Russia [Belarus], is sitting there. He has come to acquaintances he has here. They are glad to see him again. The inhabitants of the house inquire after fellow townsmen. He sighs deeply, sits down depressed and begins, slowly and with sighs, to recount those things that weigh so heavily on the spirit and which reawaken half-forgotten bloody memories. One thousand five hundred Jews of Braslav were shot dead in the streets. The whole time, he says, we had lived as good neighbours with the Christians, with the White Russian peasants. They helped us, until the orders came and our own peasant neighbours, together with the Germans, killed off all the Jews of the town. Their property was plundered, slashed, torn, everything smashed and scattered. A few Jews, he among them, ran from the pit. He wandered over roads and forests. The whole Belarusian earth is [soaked] in Jewish blood, he cries out. The people in the room ask about one town or another in the White Russian region. "No more, no more," he replies with such a sad voice. The White Russian Jewish towns were cut down as with a scythe. As quietly as a candle, Jewish life was bloodily snuffed out in them ...

He seems to be an urban, middle-class Jew. He cries out, bursting into tears: "Oh, we have been so uprooted in Belarus, oh, oh, how uprooted. Torn limb from limb. I don't have any reason to go back to Braslav after the war. It's enough that I have lost everyone there, my wife and children. Just one thing, I'll go to see the revenge, the revenge on those who cut us down."

Thursday, 14 [January 1943]. Today the ghetto is on edge again. Especially, as it happens, the workers at the *Schneiderstube*. For a change, Murer has caused a misfortune. New victims have fallen into his jaws. The singer Lyuba Levitska was coming from the *Schneiderstube* together with another person, carrying peas into the ghetto. Then Murer arrived and ordered them to stand still. They ran off. With a revolver in hand, he caught them and asked them where they were coming from. Levitska answered that she is coming from the kitchen of the *Schneiderstube*, where she works. Murer ordered the Jewish police to give each of them twenty-five lashes with wet towels. All bloodied, they were taken to Lukishki Prison, from which people seldom return. Murer, a raging devil, rushed off to the *Schneiderstube* to tell the workers. There he raged like a storm. First he ran to the pot where they cook (to establish if Levitska told him the truth). The cooks, in a panic, lifted the lids off the pots and the room filled with steam; people couldn't see one another. Crazy Murer screams: "Light!" They bring him matches. The matches won't light in the steam. Driven mad by anger, he asks the cook, the Jew, what they are cooking. The Jew answers: "I swear on my holy oath, only barley and potatoes." Murer beat up the Jew, then threw himself with an axe on two Jews who were sawing wood. That is how he rampaged, insulted and tortured ... The ghetto is completely upset. Levas said that if he had been there, those two people would not have gone to jail. He would have whipped their faces, satisfying Murer with their blood, and they would have remained in the ghetto. Murer would not have pulled them out. With blood you can easily quench his thirst to torment and to torture. It may be that Levas is right, but how terrible and how sad our life is, how helpless and how exposed to perils and torments we are ...

Sunday, 17 [January 1943]. A cold wave is upon us. Winter has arrived, the brute, greatest enemy of the people of the ghetto. People walk around frozen. Few homes are well heated. Today I didn't feel good and didn't go to the Club.

Thursday, 22 [actually 21 January 1943]. Today my father went off to do unskilled labour. He has been laid off from the *Schneiderstube.* The cold wave has broken. The streets have thawed. I am alone at home. I had a lot of work today. I did the cooking.

Friday, 22 [January 1943]. Today is a school holiday – *Khamishe-oser bi-Shvat.* Included in the program was a performance by the young members of the Children's Club.

Sunday, 24 [January 1943]. Today a general meeting of the Club took place. The discussion about the Club, about its future activities, lasted late into the night. I am of the opinion that things are not in order at the Club right now. The performances of the dramatic circle have too much influence in the Club. The other circles have almost ceased to be a place for serious work. At the meeting, all of this was debated.

Monday, 25 [January 1943]. The frost hit us hard again. It's cold in the classroom. Everyone stands around the little stove, holding their frozen fingers out near the pipes. Nevertheless, it's cheerful and lively there. When you study, you don't feel the cold. The windows of the classroom are frozen, encased in ice. We keep adding more and more wood to the stove. But the wood is wet and the students have to blow without stopping. We go to the Club. The walls are covered with ice. A circle is about to begin meeting. I run to light a fire in the stove.

Wednesday, 27 [January 1943]. Today we visited, with the Club, the ghetto workshops at 6 Rudnitsker Street. There, at 6 Rudnitsker Street, is concentrated the entire ghetto industry. Here our skilled workers work, which is the basis of our existence. The ghetto has exerted all its power to create what we saw here today. We go from section to section – the locksmiths, the mechanics, the tinsmiths. There is banging and clanging. Everything bears the stamp of serious work. They repair the parts of machines. And here they produce iron badges with numbers on them which every Jew, like a cow, will wear around his neck. Here is a forge with two burners. The air here is warm, filled with the heat of iron and lime. The fires blaze in the dark ovens and the Jews stand silently, banging monotonously with their hammers. The Jewish blacksmith stands and makes horseshoes for the German military. In the courtyard they are building a big forge with six burners. We go into another section. We are led by an angry, strict engineer who yells at the workers like a boss. Murer's orders have spread everywhere ... Only the specialist workers are not impressed by the engineer, because they know they are needed. Murer already knows them and he will not replace them with others. Just now a worker cursed the engineer who is leading us for starting up a machine without his permission ... Here is the section of wood lathes, for the wooden-sole industry. How beautiful, how enticing is the work, the woodcutting, as things are created before my very eyes. But for whom? ... Here are the rooms for furniture manufacture. They have a history of their own in the ghetto. Hingst, Murer, the *Gebietskommissare* of Vilna order furniture here. The most beautiful sets of furniture are made here. Women stand and polish the beautiful pieces of furniture. Some children inadvertently throw out a lath. "Children," says a worker, "our dear friend Murer will come and make a scene." Murer comes very often to the workshops. The workshops then are engulfed in painful fear. It turns deathly quiet. Only the tools seem to say, nervously: "Murer is coming." And he appears in the workshops like a calamity, like a storm, like a crazed beast of prey. He orders the workers to do gymnastics and with good reason the workers practise every day and climb under the table and on top of the table ... Everything is done here silently, with clenched teeth. There is no singing at work ... Now a new section is being built, where the only specialist, a Vilna Jew, will make artificial hand and feet. "Let's hope this section has a lot of orders," people quip.

Everything I saw here was created only through will

On exiting the workshops I was left with the impression of the strength of the will to life that is emitted by everything here. Everything I saw here was created only through will. Alone in the ghetto street I think who will benefit from our work and the products of our work – wolves and dogs. But our will to live, as I saw it today, very clearly announces that the sombre game will come to an end, that finally that spectre named Murer will disappear. "You should be workers and not oppressors," a blacksmith said to us today. Yes, we will be workers, but we will be working in different times.

I am now reading Alexander Avdeyenko's book *I Love*.
The book made a strong impression on me with its honesty and
the humanity which arises from it.

Thursday, 28 [January 1943]. The hope that is continually alive
among the ghetto inhabitants has lately flared up. The proud
German war bulletins become, alas, like women's prayers. The
German war communiqué admits to a powerful Soviet offensive
on all fronts. The Soviets have begun a great offensive in the sector between the Caucasus and the Don. The victorious German
army which had threatened Stalingrad and made it into its suburbs
has been caught in a mighty encirclement by the Soviet armies.
The Soviet armoured divisions are driving the Germans out of the
Caucasus. The Germans are threatened with a huge defeat on this
front. In Stalingrad, where the German army battled so might-
ily, they have battled their way into the grave. The German attack
on Stalingrad has turned into a desperate resistance by encircled
forces. "The German soldier displays an iron heart against the flood
of iron" – so says today's bulletin. Yes, they confess that a flood of
Soviet armament is upon them, that the Soviets are stronger. They
console themselves with the heroism and discipline of the German
soldier, but we know better which soldiers are greater heroes. It gives
my heart a warm feeling: the Soviet offensive drives across the front
and soon it will come to us, bearing the flame of freedom.

In the evening, I went to an interesting session of the literary circle. The young poet A. Sutskever told us about the Yiddish poet Yehoash. We read his poems. The description of nature in Yehoash's poems truly inspired us. Yehoash's theme, which was beauty in sun and mist, is indeed so pleasing. Reading Yehoash we are united with beauty. In his poems, Yehoash presents nature in all its splendour. We have decided to organise a Yehoash evening with a Yehoash exhibition. Sutzkever has succeeded, while working at YIVO, in salvaging many valuable items, such as letters and manuscripts.

Friday, 29 [January 1943]. Today the ghetto is saddened by the news that Lyuba Levitska and Stupel, who were recently detained, have been shot in the prison. Until now, it was still believed that it would be possible to free them. They say that Lyuba used to sing for the prison guards in order to obtain a piece of bread. She sang among the prison cells until her life was cut short. A talent has disappeared.

Thursday, 4 February [1943]. In the ghetto there is a new turmoil. Murer visited Fryd, "the Ghetto President", and found that he had at his place 4 kilograms of candy. Murer detained Frid. The whole ghetto is furious at this old snob who used to sit in his office as if on a throne, with candy at his side. People are afraid he might blurt something about the ghetto to Murer. In the evening Frid was brought back and immediately fired from his position.

Sunday, 7 February [1943]. There is good news. The people of the ghetto are jubilant. The Germans have admitted that Stalingrad has fallen.

I walk along the street … People wink to each other with happiness in their eyes. Finally the Germans have been dealt a gigantic defeat. The whole German Ninth Army is shattered. Over 300,000 Germans killed. The General Staff taken prisoner. Stalin's city, the enemy's grave. The Soviet winter offensive is delivering brilliant results.

I walk in the street. Winter is already departing from the ghetto streets. The air is warm and sunny. The ice in the streets is melting and running and my heart is so springlike. Inside us the snow is melting and our hearts are feeling so sunny. The liberation is coming; I feel in my blood how close it is.

Sunday, 14 [February 1943]. Things are good, things are joyful. The Soviet offensive is proceeding outstandingly. Kharkov and Rostov have been captured. Goebbels, the German propaganda minister, gave a speech filled with pessimism. We were delighted with his calls for help – he appeals to all cultured nations to help Germany against the Soviets, because things are in a bad way.

This time Goebbels has uttered a great truth, that if the German front collapses, Bolshevism will inundate the world. And he is not ashamed to say that the German front is about to collapse and they have to exert all their strength so that it doesn't go kaput.

Sunday, 27 February [actually 28 February 1943]. Today I had an exceptional day. In the last two weeks much that is new has been added to my life. Some fifteen of us have begun in the ghetto a P. [Pioneer] activity. We are led by Teacher M [Mire Bernshteyn] and Comrade Mu [Musye Saginar]. We discussed whether in general we need such an undertaking in the ghetto. We came to the conclusion that yes, we do. Our work will consist of being the vanguard for the rest of our friends; we have to bring the others along with us, we have to see to it that there is good common social life in the Club and in school. At our meetings we will also work on ourselves, because we have to prepare for the life that awaits us. The future will require conscientious people who will have to lead the masses in the great reconstruction. Our first requirement for such work is discipline and conspiracy. For the first time I now sense what it means to work in secret. We haven't yet fully devoted ourselves to this work, but we are getting used to it. Up to today we have been meeting in nooks. One time we were locked in the dark in the Club. For today we have prepared a celebration in honour of the twenty-fifth anniversary of the Red Army, which fell on Tuesday the 23rd. In our nooks we have collected money among ourselves, and potatoes and beets for a communal glass of tea. Each of us grasps the importance of the work and the responsibilities that come with it. Finally, we will have our celebration today. No place has been found yet. We had agreed on the Club. The secretary of the Club, one of our own people, had promised to arrange it. At the last minute, we transferred to the home of an older comrade. The conspiracy is great. Our boys are standing at the Club and at the comrade's gate. One by one we move over there. At last, the salad arrives. Bread and cookies are brought in as a present from the older comrades. And here we are sitting in a room. The people in the room are our own people. There stands a salad in the form of a star and Stalin's picture stands next to it. The door is locked, but then Teacher M and several of our own people come in. I open the celebration. I greet the ceremonial Pioneer gathering dedicated to the twenty-fifth anniversary of the Red Army, our dear friend whom we await and of whose victory we are certain. The mood is elevated. I sense that we are being reunited with the life that we were temporarily torn away from. We sing Soviet songs, comrades read what they have written about the Red Army and its leaders. We now all live fused together in the love of the Red Army, in the love of Soviet life. Teacher Op [Opeskin] reads his poems written for the Soviets: "To the Red Tank Gunner".

The wishes of our parents are that we should ride on the victorious Red tanks over the liberated streets. We, Pioneers, feel that way too. We read Stalin's Order of the Day under the heading: "Death to the Occupier!" Thus in the ghetto, on February 28th we celebrated, joyously and intimately, the twenty-fifth anniversary of the Red Army. We depart one by one. From our souls cries out: for its recent victories – passionate greetings to the Red Army. Long Live the Red Army!

Sunday, 7 March [1943]. Today the trial of Flavius Josephus, a hero of the time of the Destruction of the Second Temple, took place in the Club, arranged by the circle of Jewish history. I was a witness, Yokhanan of Gush Khalav, a famous hero and a leader of the Zealots. The trial was quite interesting, but it went on for too long.

Wednesday, 10 March [1943]. Spring is more and more in evidence in the ghetto. The sun gives warmth. Against the walls, where it's sunny, people are standing with children and the children turn their pale little faces towards the sun. Every day I am busy all day. In the morning – in school. In the afternoon – homework. I am busy with housekeeping. In the evening, with P. gatherings and at the Club. At the P. gatherings we now talk about the national question. We have also received a review of the Soviet communiqués about the winter offensive. It has become clear to us that the Soviets are moving boldly forward, have taken Stalingrad, Kharkov, Rostov and tens of other points. The attack goes forward on the Don–Caucasus sector. The Red Army has reached a point 50 kilometres from the Dnieper. The Red Army is also attacking on the first front in the direction of Velikie Luki, towards Riga. The Soviet Union is now cooperating with England against their common enemy, but the Soviets stand solidly alone in the battle. They carry the entire war in the east on their shoulders.

We are meeting, for the time being, at the home of a female comrade. In the Club we are also working to prepare a Yehoash evening. I have written a composition: "Reading Yehoash in the Ghetto". In the evenings we prepare with Kh. [*Khaver* – friend, comrade] Sutskever, who is directing the project, a superb exhibition. Sutzkever has brought many important materials from YIVO – manuscripts, books, photographs. We will display this in a beautiful Yehoash exhibition. We have also created a beautiful Yehoash newspaper. The preparations for the Yehoash celebration are proceeding at a rapid pace.

Thursday, 11 [March 1943]. I was at the Club till late at night. We are preparing for the superb Yehoash evening. I haven't been getting enough sleep.

Sunday, 14 March [1943]. Today there took place in the Club the Yehoash celebration and the opening of the Yehoash exhibition. The exhibition is exceptionally beautiful. The whole reading room in the Club is decorated with material. It is well lit and tidy and your eyes light up when you go in. For this exhibition we have Kh. Sutskever to thank. From YIVO, where he works, he was able to smuggle in a lot of material for the Yehoash exhibition. When you go into the exhibition, you see the youthful energy which gave full vent to everything here. Everything was selected in a beautiful and youthful way. Everything is so cultural and full of warmth. People came in here and forgot that they were in the ghetto. We have here in the exhibition many valuable documents that now are treasures. Manuscripts sent from Peretz to Yehoash, Yehoash's handwritten letters. We have rare newspaper clippings. In the section "*Tanakh* Translations into Yiddish", we have old Yiddish *Tanakh* translations from the seventeenth century. Looking at the exhibition, at our work, your heart fills up with pride and enthusiasm. You really do forget that we are in a sombre ghetto. The celebration today also went splendidly. The dramatic circle presented Yehoash's dramatic scene "Saul". Club members read their essays about Yehoash's writings, about Yehoash the poet of beauty, sound and colour. The mood at the celebration was lofty; it really was a holiday, a demonstration of Yiddish literature and culture.

Tuesday, 16 [March 1943]. Today news came in from town. The editor of the Polish newspaper *Goniec*, that hooligan, was shot dead in church. This deed by Vilna Poles pleased me greatly. In all of Lithuania mass arrests took place in high places. They say that the Lithuanians have issued a manifesto refusing to be mobilised until the Germans have granted them independence.

Thursday, 18 [March 1943]. I am busy for hours on end. It is so hard to make time for school and the Club and then to get entangled in cooking and cleaning. First of all, school presentations have cropped up. In school, in geography, we are working on the theme of Vilna. I have to present the topic "On Jewish Printing in Vilna". For the last several months there has been no lighting in the evening, so we hang around in the workroom, in the reading room. I often think: this is supposed to be the ghetto, yet I have such a full life of cultural activity: I study, I read, visit the Club circles. Time flies by so fast and there is so much work to do. Lectures, [cultural] evenings. I often forget that I am in the ghetto.

Friday, 19 [March 1943]. We had a P. meeting. There is news that is not so good for us. The G.F. [*Geto-forshteyer*, ghetto chief Jacob Gens] called a meeting where he stated that the youth in the ghetto are not being raised in the appropriate national spirit.

It was the Z. [Zionists] who prompted him. It is painful when I think how such coarse types talk about our education. Up till now the internal front in the ghetto has been a common one. Now we are on the brink of a split. The blows against us can come from our own brother. We're at the point where the clumsy policemen's paw might come down on our development. But we will endure – and will strengthen our conspiracy.

Saturday, 20 [March 1943]. We have been freed [from school] for three days – a Purim break. The three days were very useful. I did something about my pile of presentations. In the street it is springtime. I sit in the courtyard of 6 Rudnitsker Street. The sun is shining and warms and caresses. The air is breezy and springlike. The sky is blue. It smells of spring. Spring forces its way over the grey walls, comes into the ghetto and bears on its caressing rays, on the blue air, the message that somewhere things are already turning green, somewhere willows are blooming, somewhere birds are already tweeting. And I delight in the spring breeze, catch the spring rays and my heart is drawn away somewhere ...

Sunday, 21 March [1943]. There was a gathering dedicated to the anniversary of the Paris C. [Commune]. A comrade gave a talk: "The Communards, the Eternal Example for the Fighting Proletariat".

In the evening we had a Purim celebration in the Club. We felt the urge for it, so then let it be Purim. We were the ones who set the tone. We sang songs and presented a [satirical] Purim play: "Leo (our manager) the Patriarch and the Twelve Sections of the Club". Comrade Shmerke [Kaczerginski] sang with us and Pilnik, our theatre manager, who was slightly drunk, chimed in. He laughed a lot, then went home to bed. We are awaiting the real Purim next year, when we will eat Hitler-tashen.

Thursday, 25 March [1943]. An order was issued by the German authorities concerning the liquidation of five small ghettos in the Vilna region. The Jews are being transferred to the Vilna and Kovno ghettos. Today the Jews from the neighbouring small towns are already beginning to arrive. In the street it is rainy and grey. The peasant carts sadly enter the ghetto like Gypsy covered wagons. On the carts sit Jews with children and their bags and baggage. The newly arrived Jews have to be provided with places to live. The school at 1 Shavler Street has been taken over for the newly arrived Jews. The school at 1 Shavler Street has moved into the building of our school. Classes are held in two shifts. Today we already went to class in the evening. School doesn't make any sense. All of us are depressed. The mood is gloomy.

Sunday, 28 [March 1943]. The mood in the ghetto is very oppressive. Squeezing so many Jews into one place is a signal of something. Bringing food through the gate has become very difficult. Several people have already been arrested and sent to Lukishki Prison. People go around grey and preoccupied. Danger lurks in the air. No! This time we will not let ourselves be led like dogs to slaughter! We have been talking about this lately at our [Pioneer meetings]. We are ready for every moment. We have to work on ourselves. This thought strengthens our nerves, restores our courage and endurance.

Sunday, 4 [April 1943]. But our group does not let the bad mood take over. Every Sunday we have some form of amusement in the Club. Today there was an interesting quiz evening. We sang and had fun as young people usually do.

Monday, 5 [April 1943]. Sunday at three o'clock the streets were closed off in the ghetto. A group of 300 people, from the Jews of Sol and Smorgon, went away to Kovno on a large transport. A transport of Jews from the region had arrived at the railway station. Standing at the gate, I could see them packing. Happily and in a good mood they went to the train. Today we received the terrifying news: eighty-five railway cars of Jews, about 5000 people, were not taken to Kovno as they had been promised, but were taken by train to Ponar, where they were shot to death. Five thousand new bloody victims. The ghetto was profoundly shaken, as if struck by a thunderclap. The mood of massacre has taken hold of the population. It has begun again. The claws of the hawk have appeared before us again. People sit confined in a crate and on the other side lurks the enemy, who is preparing to annihilate us in a refined way according to a plan, as today's massacre has shown. The ghetto is dejected and saddened. We are defenceless and faced with death. Once again the nightmare of Ponar hovers over the little ghetto streets. It is terrible, terrible. People are walking around like the living dead. They wring their hands. In the evening an urgent meeting: the situation is clear-cut. We have no one to rely on. The danger is very great. We have confidence in our own strength. We are ready at any minute.

Tuesday, 6 [April 1943]. The situation is oppressive. All the terrifying details are now already known. Instead of to Kovno, 5000 Jews were taken to Ponar, where they were shot dead. Like wild animals faced with death they began as a matter of life and death to break out of the railway cars. They broke the little windows that were fortified with strong wires. Hundreds of Jews were shot while running away. The railway lines are covered with the dead for a long stretch. There were no classes in school today. Children are running away from their homes where it is terrible to remain because of the mood there, because of the women. At school the teachers are devastated as well. So we sit in a circle. We pull ourselves together. We sing a song.

In the evening I go out into the street. It is five o'clock in the afternoon. The ghetto looks dreadful. Heavy leaden clouds move over the ghetto and envelop it. It is dark like before a storm. Our mood, like the sky, is overcast. The streets are filled with people, lost and frightened.

Twenty-five policemen were taken to clear away the dead from the pits. Many survivors have escaped from Ponar. Here comes a Jew and after him a crowd of people. He is pale, with wild eyes. His coat is entirely covered with lime. Here they are leading in three children brought by peasants. Wounded are being brought in. It keeps getting darker. Suddenly, thunder and lightning and it starts to rain. The anxious, unhappy people are driven off the couple of little streets with whips. The rain pours angrily, as if it wished to wash everything away from the world.

At any moment, the worst can happen to us

At night I am at the Club. It is dark. The lights won't come on until nine o'clock. So we sit in the dark. The group sings a song. It feels oppressive and painful. The situation is still very tense. We are on guard. Yes, that very thought relieves the difficult hours.

Wednesday [7 April 1943]. The mood has improved a little. In the Club you can already hear a happy little song. But we are prepared for everything, because Monday has revealed that we must trust nobody, believe nobody. At any moment, the worst can happen to us. ▤

Subscribe to The Jewish Quarterly and save.

Enjoy free delivery of The Jewish Quarterly to your door, digital access to every issue of The Jewish Quarterly for one year, and exclusive special offers.

Never miss an issue.
Subscribe and save.

- 1 year* print and digital subscription (4 issues) £55 GBP | $75 USD
- 1 year* digital subscription (4 issues) £35 GBP | $45 USD

Subscribe now:

Visit **jewishquarterly.com/subscribe**

Email **subscribe@jewishquarterly.com**

Scan one of these QR codes with your mobile device camera app:

Subscribe in £GBP   Subscribe in $USD